THE STUDENTS OF SHERMAN INDIAN SCHOOL

THE STUDENTS OF SHERMAN INDIAN SCHOOL

Education and Native Identity since 1892

Diana Meyers Bahr

University of Oklahoma Press : Norman

Also by Diana Meyers Bahr

From Mission to Metropolis: Cupeño Indian Women in Los Angeles
(Norman, Okla., 1993)

Viola Martinez, California Paiute: Living in Two Worlds
(Norman, Okla., 2003)

The Unquiet Nisei: An Oral History of the Life of Sue Kunitomi Embrey
(New York, 2007)

Library of Congress Cataloging-in-Publication Data

Bahr, Diana Meyers, 1930–
The students of Sherman Indian School: education and native identity since 1892 / Diana Meyers Bahr.
    pages   cm
Includes bibliographical references and index.
ISBN 978-0-8061-4443-6 (pbk.: alk. paper)
1. Sherman Indian High School (Riverside, Calif.) 2. Indian children—Education. 3. Off-reservation boarding schools—History. I. Title.
E97.6.S54B34 2013
373.794'97—dc23
                             2013030745

The paper in this book meets the guidelines for permanence and durability of the Committee on Production Guidelines for Book Longevity of the Council on Library Resources, Inc. ∞

Copyright © 2014 by the University of Oklahoma Press, Norman, Publishing Division of the University. Manufactured in the U.S.A.

All rights reserved. No part of this publication may be reproduced, stored in a retrieval system, or transmitted, in any form or by any means, electronic, mechanical, photocopying, recording, or otherwise—except as permitted under Section 107 or 108 of the United States Copyright Act—without the prior written permission of the University of Oklahoma Press. To request permission to reproduce selections from this book, write to Permissions, University of Oklahoma Press, 2800 Venture Drive, Norman, OK 73069, or email rights.oupress@ou.edu.

Contents

List of Illustrations	vii
Acknowledgments	ix
Introduction: The Complicated Middle Course	3
1. Assimilation Imposed, Self-Determination Promised, 1892–1933	15
2. Reform, War, and Innovation, 1934–1952	43
3. Termination—"Tragedy" and "Challenge," 1953–1972	73
4. Red Power and Self-Determination, 1973–2000	89
5. Self-Determination and At-Risk Students, 2001–2012	117
Conclusion: Forgiving the Past	135
Notes	141
Bibliography	157
Index	169

Illustrations

All photographs are provided courtesy of the Sherman Indian Museum and are reproduced here with permission of the Curator. Because many of the photographs were archived without dates, the decades given in the captions are best guesses.

Perris Indian School, Perris, California, 1900	36
Sherman Institute building, constructed in 1901	36
Riverside campus dormitory, constructed by 1908	37
Ramona dormitory for older boys	37
Romaldo La Chusa, member of first graduating class in 1904	38
Class of 1904, Perris Indian School	39
Grade school girls at Perris Indian School, 1908	39
Grade school boys at Perris Indian School, 1908	40
Girls on Sherman Institute's Riverside campus	40
Sherman Indian Museum	41
Sherman Indian High School campus, 2013	41
Sherman Indian High School modernized campus, 2013	42
Navajo students in special five-year program	108
Boys working on Sherman ranch, 1930s	109
Girls working on Sherman ranch, 1940s	109

Students in the outing system	110
Sherman campus bakery	111
Boys making bread in campus bakery, 1930s	111
Sherman girls in Rural Home Life Course	112
Student mechanics working on ranch machinery, 1946	112
Boys doing carpentry	113
Sherman Band	113
Classroom, 1963	114
Harold Nading, Sherman administrator, 1962–75	114
Roland Doepner, English teacher and principal	115
Lorene Sisquoc, cultural traditions director and museum curator	115

Acknowledgments

NO ONE CAN WRITE ABOUT SHERMAN INDIAN SCHOOL without the invaluable help of Lorene Sisquoc, curator of the Sherman Indian Museum and cultural traditions leader of the school. This history of Sherman would not have been completed without the committed participation of Lorene. I am appreciative of the support of Clifford E. Trafzer, who provided not only scholarly and practical advice but also sympathetic encouragement. Matthew Sakiestewa Gilbert composed a significantly thorough and perceptive peer review. His comments on the manuscript added important insights, especially in regard to Native American traditions.

I especially value those who shared their unique memories of Sherman: Galen Townsend, Tonita Largo Glover, Lorene Sisquoc, Michele Meyers Conejo, Willetta Davis Goins, Jason Davis, Melvin Campbell, Gary Evans, and Robert Evans. Dr. Elwin Svenson enriched the section on the Kennedy report on Indian education with personal accounts of his evaluation of Sherman.

I am very pleased to have the University of Oklahoma Press once more as publisher of my work. Alessandra Jacobi-Tamulevich was encouraging and pragmatic and especially helpful in structuring an effective organization for the book. I am deeply grateful to Steven B. Baker, who was consistently accessible, while being an expert editor. I am extremely impressed with and thankful for freelance copy editor Sally Bennett, who, with meticulous and intelligent editing, rescued my manuscript from numerous errors and enhanced the flow of the text.

Once again, I am indebted to Linda Stowe, not only for her excellent transcribing of the tapes of oral interviews but also for her keen interest in the BIA Brats. Kara Schwab and Matthew Townsend provided information about Sherman sports, for which I am grateful. My treatment of sports in Sherman's history is far from complete. The significance of sports in Sherman's history warrants a book of its own, a fertile topic for further research.

I am truly appreciative of my husband, Ted, who was intelligently and sympathetically supportive, remaining unruffled during my outbursts of frustration and angst and saving me from a meltdown when my computer mouse froze.

THE STUDENTS OF SHERMAN INDIAN SCHOOL

Introduction

The Complicated Middle Course

ON OCTOBER 9, 2010, during the 107th annual alumni reunion of Sherman Institute (which later became Sherman Indian High School), as I sat in the small museum library, crammed with books and documents, I was captivated by the alumni and students who reverently looked up relatives and friends in the yearbooks of the school. One young man was talking on his cell phone with his mother while conscientiously searching through the yearbooks for names she was conveying to him. This encounter was one of many that convinced me of the attachment former students have for Sherman Institute. Even alumni whose memories are depressing or ambivalently fond and regretful retain an undeniable attachment to the school. Their deeply felt experience is characteristic in the history of federal boarding schools, a history dating back to 1879, in which complex emotions and powerful memories are pervasive.

Sherman Institute opened in Perris, California, in 1892, a time of intense focus on assimilating Indians into mainstream society. The last of twenty-five federal off-reservation boarding schools to be opened, Sherman had the fourth largest enrollment and the fifth largest average attendance. It currently is one of the four remaining off-reservation boarding schools: the other three are Riverside Indian School in Oklahoma, Chemawa Indian School in Oregon, and Flandreau Indian School in South Dakota.[1]

Education of Indian youths, however, did not begin with schools established by whites. The pursuit of knowledge has always been a significant force in the lives of Indian people. Knowledge, both sacred and practical, and accrued over thousands of years, has formed the foundation of their cultures. The first teachers of Indian children were their families and clans.[2] Tribal elders were responsible for introducing children to knowledgeable men and women for instruction in behavior and respect for tribal traditions and histories, as well as for emphasizing correct behavior to individual children who had erred.[3]

Native educators stress that "formal" education means more than schools: K. Tsianina Lomawaima and Teresa L. McCarty in *To Remain an Indian: Lessons in Democracy from a Century of Native American Education* argue, "Because the school = formal education is so powerful, Native education usually has been equated with *informal*, since Indigenous education over the last five centuries has usually occurred 'out of school' ... but close examination reveals that all educational systems incorporate both formal and informal aspects." With illustrations from Indian autobiographies, the authors examine patterns within Indigenous education: instruction for strength, education according to gender, according to age, for leadership, and according to clan or rank. They describe how Native education is embedded in names, songs, and stories. They claim that catechism, the question-and-answer exchange between teacher and student, is "not foreign to Native educational systems." Moreover, they state, "In addition to songs, stories and catechism, Native caregivers marshaled language through lectures, directions, encouragement, and scolding to shape children's thoughts and behaviors." They illuminate how Indian children learn by observation, how they learn in the home, and how plants and animals are teachers. They conclude by advocating a return to choice and local control and affirming that indigenous knowledge and education systems have proved resilient.[4]

Relying on Indian autobiographical accounts, historian Michael C. Coleman concludes that students at Carlisle Indian Boarding School did not have either/or responses to the alternating periods of assimilation and self-determination in the Indian education policies of the federal government. He believes they fit the concept of ambivalence as a dynamic state as formulated by anthropologist Christopher Boehm: experiencing conflicting feelings, people can blend their ambivalence in myriad ways, depending on their cultural and social experience and the situation.[5]

My research also shows that during the alternating periods of assimilation and self-determination, most Sherman students did not conform totally to either. David Treuer, an Ojibwe from Leech Lake Reservation, writes, "An Indian community muddles its way through the 21st century in something other than extreme poverty or extreme wealth, trying to make ends meet and getting the job done, engaging in all sorts of fierce moral skirmishes in the vast American middle. I think it is in response to a complicated middle . . . that action can be born. And these are the stories we are waiting for."[6] The stories of Sherman students recount struggles through the complicated middle course, engaging in powerful moral confrontations.

There are numerous concepts in the literature regarding Indian-white relations similar to the "middle course," notably, "cultural broker" and "middle ground." Historian Margaret Connell Szasz's model of cultural broker may be defined as facilitating the cultural border crossing of another person or group. Szasz asserts that cultural brokers changed roles at will, that they chose to move into an intermediary position, setting the pattern for those who followed moving between two worlds.[7]

Szasz also maintains that cultural brokers have often moved in the "middle ground" explored by historian Richard White in 1991 in *The Middle Ground: Indians, Empires, and Republics in the Great Lakes Region, 1650–1815*.[8] White describes his book as "a search for accommodation and common meaning" among Indians and whites in the Great Lakes region.[9] White's perception of the middle ground is "the place in between cultures, peoples, and empires" (x). He argues that people of diverse cultures adjusted their differences through what he calls "creative misunderstandings" (x). Indians and whites tried to manipulate each other by appealing to what they perceived were the others' values and practices, but misunderstandings occurred. From these misunderstandings arose new, shared meanings and practices on the middle ground (xv). When Indians ceased to have the power to force whites onto the middle ground and whites began to dictate the terms of accommodation, the middle ground eroded. White's work challenges the belief that whites were the overpowering assailants and Indians were puppet victims.[10]

In 1992, historian Daniel H. Usner, Jr., wrote about a similar middle ground in what he called the "frontier exchange economy" of settlers and slaves in the lower Mississippi valley in the late eighteenth century.[11] "Frontier exchange" refers to the economic interaction of Indians in the lower Mississippi valley with European settlers and African slaves along the Gulf Coast and the lower banks of the Mississippi River (6). The frontier exchange evolved from the interaction among the three groups into a strategy for economic survival (8). The plantation system began to replace the frontier economy, but the economic practices of this frontier persisted into the nineteenth century (9).

Richard White is credited with being in the forefront of the "New Western History" and establishing a meaningful new framework for the study of Indian-white relations.[12] The middle ground theory, however, is not new in historiography. Some scholars, such as Bradley J. Birzer, have traced the intellectual seeds of the middle ground as far back as Frederick Jackson Turner's 1893 renowned essay, "The Significance of the Frontier in American History."[13] Birzer argues that one can discover in Turner's essay "at least one half of the middle ground concept" (3). He asserts that the middle ground concept remakes "Turner's one-sided frontier into a multisided frontier in which cultures merge, accommodate, resist, and create" (1). Historian Wilbur R. Jacobs asserts that the middle ground theory represents "a certain 'cross fertilization' of Turnerian frontier thought, ethnohistory, and the 'New Western History.'"[14]

There is indeed perhaps some evidence in Turner's essay of the intellectual seeds of the middle ground theory: "We note that the frontier promoted the formation of a composite nationality.... Interstate migration went steadily on—a process of cross-fertilization of ideas and institutions ... breaking the bond of custom, offering new experience, calling out new institutions and activities, that and more, the ever retreating frontier has been to the United States."[15]

Federal Indian boarding schools historically have been a unique middle ground. Lomawaima and McCarty describe this education environment as a "safety zone." Their theory raises questions about the middle ground occupied by Indian students and Indian education policy: "Which native beliefs and practices might be judged safe, innocuous and tolerable? Which beliefs and practices are too dangerous, different, and subversive of mainstream values? How best to manage or eradicate dangerous cultural expressions?" Their premise refers to the efforts of the federal government to determine whether certain Native cultural expressions were "safe," according to Indian education policy.[16]

My concept of the middle course generally differs from the theories of Szasz, White, Usner, and Lomawaima and McCarty. Sherman students negotiated a middle course as a process that allowed them to cope with powerful moral confrontations. While this process may have enabled them to later act as cultural brokers, it primarily was an effort to maintain the integrity of their Native culture while making accommodations that allowed them to succeed in school. The middle course of Sherman students was dissimilar to White's middle ground in two ways: manipulating others was not an aspect of their demeanor, and the middle course did not erode. The middle course is, however, similar to the middle ground model of White in that it demonstrates that Sherman students were not passive pushovers. Rather, they made decisions and took actions that allowed them to cope with the confrontations between white and Native cultures.

The middle course of Sherman students is dissimilar to the frontier exchange theory in that their cultural exchange was between whites and Indians only and economics was not a salient factor. The students were selecting a path through painful conflicts with a white culture determined to eradicate their Native cultures. The middle course also differs from the "safety zone" of Lomawaima and McCarty; although their work recounts Indigenous resistance to federal policy, the "safety zone" concept was a policy imposed from the top down by the Bureau of Indian Affairs, whereas the middle course was a process used by Sherman students from the ground up.

Perhaps the greatest similarity with what I describe as the middle course of Sherman students is the concept of "turning the power." Historian Clifford E. Trafzer explains the term as follows: "Some students turned the power and used their boarding school days to their own advantage, creating opportunities for themselves and making use of their new knowledge to benefit their people."[17] Sherman students turned the power by navigating a middle course from the beginning of the school's history.

Sherman Institute originated as the Perris Indian School, twenty-five miles south of Riverside, which had opened in 1892, with an original population of 9 students that expanded to 150 during the first year of Sherman Institute and 500 by 1905. The 2012 population was 350 students. While doing research for her groundbreaking study *Empty Beds:*

Indian Health at Sherman Institute, 1902–1922, Jean Keller surmised that nothing had been published about Perris Indian School or Sherman Institute.[18] While nothing comprehensive about Sherman's history has been published, accounts of students' lives in this federal Indian boarding school are found in five works, in addition to Keller's book, which documents Sherman's efforts to create a healthy environment for its Indian students, who were struggling against severe diseases. *No Turning Back: A Hopi Woman's Struggle to Live in Two Worlds* (1964), as told to Vada F. Carlson by Polingaysi Qoyawayma, is the account of Qoyawayma's defiance of her parents by choosing to attend Sherman Institute and her subsequent efforts to integrate her white education with her Native values. Don Talayesva's *Sun Chief: The Autobiography of a Hopi Indian* (1970), edited by Leo W. Simmons, is the autobiography of a Hopi who attended Sherman Institute for ten years and, like Qoyawayma, struggled to reconcile the white and Native cultures. *Education beyond the Mesas: Hopi Students at Sherman Institute, 1902–1929* (2010), by Matthew Sakiestewa Gilbert, is the absorbing chronicle of generations of Hopi students who navigated their time at Sherman Institute so successfully that they retained their Native values while using their white education to help their people when they returned home. *The Indian School on Magnolia Avenue: Voices and Images of Sherman Institute* (2012), edited by Clifford E. Trafzer, Matthew Sakiestewa Gilbert, and Lorene Sisquoc, comprises several research projects on Sherman, including the nursing program, the outing program, and the participation of Sherman students in the military in World War II, among others. My oral history, *Viola Martinez: California Paiute Living in Two Worlds* (2003), devotes a chapter to Viola's in-depth narration of her life at Sherman Institute. The present volume, a study of Sherman over its hundred-year history, is the only comprehensive portrayal of the school.

The federal Indian off-reservation boarding school system has a history of more than 130 years. Prominent in this history is Richard Henry Pratt, who had a long military career in the Tenth U.S. Cavalry during the so-called Indian Wars on the western and southern plains. Subsequent to active service, he experimented at Fort Marion in Saint Augustine, Florida, with educating Indian prisoners who had surrendered at the end of the Red River War in 1875. Inspired by the success of establishing classes in English, math, and Christianity, he secured the approval of the federal government to establish the Carlisle Indian Industrial School in Carlisle, Pennsylvania, in 1879. Although Carlisle was founded on the infamous philosophy that the government must "kill the Indian to save the man," evaluations of Pratt's policy vary from cultural genocide to forward thinking for his time, in regarding Indians as worthy of respect and being capable of participation in white society. While most of his contemporaries deemed Indians as too inferior to be successfully educated, Pratt believed that all people, including Indians, had the ability to improve through education.[19]

Carlisle became the model for future Indian boarding schools, administered by the Bureau of Indian Affairs (BIA), with a half day of classes and a half day of manual labor, which is the structure employed by Sherman throughout most of its 120-year history. Thomas Jefferson Morgan, commissioner of Indian Affairs from 1889 to 1893, following Pratt's pioneering work, became the architect of the federal government's policy for the education of Indian children. On December 1, 1889, Morgan submitted to the secretary of the Interior his comprehensive plan based on the belief, similar to that of Pratt, that education was the only salvation for Indians. Morgan perceived the Indian boarding schools as "rescuing the children and youth from barbarism and savagery."[20]

The principal rationale for the Office of Indian Education Programs, the governing agency of all BIA schools, was the need to "civilize" Indian children, who would eventually guide their people to become "refined, cultured citizens." The civilizing process required the destruction of Native cultural foundations. Indian students were isolated from their families and traditions in the off-reservation boarding schools. The component of vocational training in Indian education was designed to prepare students for economic self-sufficiency in white society. The belief that Indians were capable of becoming "civilized" prevailed for two decades but after 1900 was supplanted by the perception of Indians' inferiority. Indian education placed more emphasis on vocational training, based on the conviction that Indians needed to be taught how to work. Military discipline permeated boarding schools, resulting in a strictly regimented life with uniforms, drills, and even saluting. Students were expected to obey every rule in class, in the dormitory, and everywhere on campus. Disobedience, intentional or not, brought harsh punishment, ranging from cleaning bathrooms to having food withheld and whippings with belts.[21]

In *Boarding School Blues: Revisiting American Indian Educational Experiences,* volume editors Clifford E. Trafzer, Jean A. Keller, and Lorene Sisquoc describe how students resisted these harsh conditions and exhibited defiance of even moderate authority in many ways: not attending classes, feigning sickness, deliberately performing tasks incorrectly, "forgetting" responsibilities, even destroying campus property.[22] Hiding from authority figures in order to speak their forbidden Native languages was a frequent expression of resistance. These students were struggling to find a middle course, engaging in a dramatic moral confrontation. While many students not only adjusted to boarding school but also came to regard the school as "home," the Indian education policy had succeeded only in temporarily separating them from their culture.[23]

There were children for whom boarding school became so intolerable that they ran away. Running away from the boarding school could be viewed as the ultimate resistance, but Michael Coleman makes a distinction between resistance, which was compatible with the middle course of continued attendance, and rejection, which meant leaving the school permanently.[24] Running away was an intimidating decision. School officials often caught the runaways with the help of local police and forced them to return. Although there were rare instances of tolerance, school authorities typically resorted to severe punishment—including beatings, confinement in isolation, and humiliation—to deter runaways.[25] Parents who wanted their children to become self-sufficient in white society were also struggling with a complicated middle course and were dismayed when their children rejected the education.

Chumash youngsters Rosa Pace and her sister Beatrice Marcoe were so homesick at Sherman Institute during the 1940s that they would "meet and discuss running away." As Rosa told me, "Each time, we'd decide to wait a day or so."[26] Illustrative of the resilience, adaptation, and realistic compromise of Indian children, both Rosa and Beatrice completed their studies at the school and return annually for alumni reunions.

Homesickness was the major cause of Indian students' dropping out of boarding school. Children were separated from their families and homes and were immersed in alien surroundings with constant lining up and marching and with their days and nights regimented by the clock; in addition, they were punished for speaking their Native languages, while their cultures were being systematically demeaned. Those who did not reject the education by running away were profoundly changed, inevitably acquiring certain white attitudes and behaviors. Upon returning home, they brought these new attitudes and behaviors and became agents of change in their communities.[27]

A major component of Richard Pratt's Indian education agenda was the outing system, in which children were placed with white families and in exchange for labor would earn a small wage. Although the goal of the system was to expose Indian students to the so-called civilizing influences of white Americans, the program sometimes became exploitive, with Indian children providing a pool of cheap labor. Nevertheless, some students reported having positive experiences. They appreciated having their own money, and in some cases students and their white employers formed lasting attachments.

Jon Reyhner and Jeanne Eder describe how escalating criticism by reformers forced the federal government to rethink federal Indian policy. In 1928, the Meriam Report, which had been authorized by Hubert Work, secretary of the Interior, so severely criticized the Indian policy of the federal government that it provided justification for major change. During the Great Depression, there were significant doubts about the Indian policy, but the intensified poverty among Indian people increased enrollment in the boarding schools.[28]

Some of the findings of the Meriam Report, such as inadequate federal funding for Indian education and maintenance of the school facilities, are still relevant today. Significant gains in self-determination of Indians regarding the education of their children were made during the tenure of John Collier as commissioner of Indian Affairs, from 1933 to 1945. The Indian Reorganization Act of 1934 introduced the teaching of Indian history and culture in BIA schools. These gains were diminished during World War II when funding was constricted. The loss in education provided by schools was partly offset, however, by progress achieved in the military service and in defense work in cities.[29]

At the end of the war, the federal policy of termination and relocation focused on transferring responsibility for Indian education to individual states. This focus was consistent with the broader policy of eliminating government control by terminating health, education, and welfare assistance to tribes and sanctioning the distribution of tribal lands to individuals. By 1970, five thousand acres of tribal lands in California had been lost because individual Indians were not prepared to pay the property tax.[30] A significant feature of the termination policy was the relocation of Indians from reservations to cities, another type of forced assimilation. During these crucial shifts in federal policy, Indian education, both on and off the reservations, regressed.[31]

Education on the Navajo Reservation, in particular, was critically underfunded and undeveloped. Tribal leaders, many of whom had been exposed in the military service and defense industry to the values and working processes of white society, recognized the need for mainstream education. The BIA was motivated to create the unique Navajo Special Education Program. This innovative program adhered to some of the guidelines of the Meriam Report, including bilingual teaching.

Although the intent of this program was assimilationist, it succeeded remarkably in achieving its goals; but Indian education, including that of Sherman Institute, then declined in effectiveness because of the shifting policies of the federal government and the persistent lack of adequate funding.[32]

During the 1960s, the assertiveness of minorities captured the attention of the federal government. In the years 1967 to 1969, a major study was conducted by the Special Senate Subcommittee on Indian Education. The comprehensive study was summarized in 1969 in a report titled *Indian Education: A National Tragedy, a National Challenge*.[33] The committee was chaired by Robert Kennedy from August 28, 1967, to June 6, 1968. Edward Kennedy completed the work of his slain brother in 1969. The grim conclusions of the Kennedy Report led to a national debate on Indian education. Boarding schools, including Sherman Institute, received the harshest criticism.

Attempts to remedy the problems identified in the Kennedy Report led to a revitalization of Indian self-determination. In 1971, Sherman Institute became accredited as Sherman Indian High School. With grades nine through twelve, it is now operated by the Bureau of Indian Education and the Department of the Interior.[34] There was considerable Indian self-determination during the last three decades of the twentieth century. The Indian Self-Determination and Education Assistance Act of 1975 gave authority to federally recognized tribes to contract with the BIA for the operation of bureau-funded schools and to determine education programs for their children. The Education Amendments Act of 1978 provided funds directly to tribally operated schools, empowered Indian school boards, and permitted local hiring of teachers and staff. The first two decades of the twenty-first century have shown Native people implementing meaningful authority in Indian education. Self-determination has limits, however, and is undermined by budget cuts.

In 2006 the Office of Indian Education Programs was renamed the Bureau of Indian Education (BIE). The BIE, within the Department of the Interior, is a unique school system within the United States and a dramatic change from the BIA Indian Office days. The BIE is a federal agency that provides funding to and administers a nationwide school system. Underpinning the BIE school system is the federal trust responsibility of the government to provide educational services to schools serving American Indians. The federal government's trust responsibility to American Indian tribes is well established and has been recognized by courts, by Congress, and by the executive branch. The BIE comprises a central office in Washington, D.C.; a major field service center in Albuquerque, New Mexico; three Associate Deputy Director (ADD) offices located regionally (East, West, and Navajo); twenty-two Education Line Offices (ELO) located on or near reservations; and schools located in twenty-three states.[35]

In 2012 the BIE was responsible for educating 45,000 American Indian and Alaskan Native students in 173 elementary and secondary academic programs and in two postsecondary institutions, Haskell Indian Nations University in Lawrence, Kansas, and Southwestern Indian Polytechnic Institute in Albuquerque, New Mexico. Academic programs in BIE-funded schools conform to a variety of configurations, ranging from kindergarten alone to ninth through twelfth grades in high schools. Of the 173 BIE-funded schools, 58 (including Sherman Indian High School) are operated by the bureau, and the remaining 115 are tribally controlled. The tribally controlled schools operate under special legislation. Therefore, the BIE does not directly manage the majority of schools in its system. This fact has profound implications for sweeping reform efforts, because the BIE can only suggest that tribally controlled schools adopt key policies created for BIE schools; tribally controlled schools and school boards develop policies on their own.[36]

In Sherman Indian High School today, the curriculum includes Native language instruction, and teachers work to revive traditional skills. With sixty-eight tribes represented, students learn from each other about Indian cultural diversity. While some students attend Sherman to escape problems on the reservation, others choose the school because their grandparents, parents, other relatives, or friends attended Sherman and speak positively of it. Many students articulate their belief that federal Indian off-reservation boarding schools have a significant role in contemporary Indian life. Adequate funding is still an issue, and there is a debate within the BIA concerning whether the federal government should continue operating Indian schools in the twenty-first century.

Because of the complexity of the boarding school experience, no single interpretation is possible. Experiencing both assimilation and self-determination, students at Sherman responded by seeking a middle course and often gained a deepened appreciation of the diverse cultures of Indian America and a heightened awareness of their own Indian identity.

1

Assimilation Imposed, Self-Determination Promised

1892–1933

THE INTERIORS OF THE NINE BEAUTIFUL BUILDINGS of Spanish Mission architectural style were bare. There was no furniture, and dry goods boxes were being used for desks and for seats in the dining room. There were not enough boxes for all the students, and many had to stand during meals. The opening of Sherman Institute on September 1, 1902, was thus described by Silvas Lubo, a Cahuilla Indian, one of five children of the Lubo family enrolled as students. He described further adversity: "It was found that the money had been used up for the year and almost every employee had to be furloughed. . . . This was in March and the question came up as to what we were to do. Some of the loyal and faithful students came to the rescue. They were installed as teachers, matrons, seamstresses. The boys became heads of shops, which by the way were mostly in tents."[1]

Despite this inauspicious beginning, Sherman Institute, the last off-reservation boarding school built by the federal government, has continued to educate Indian youths for more than 120 years. The school began in 1892 as the Perris Indian School on eighty acres situated twenty-five miles south of Riverside, with an enrollment of 176 students. Entrepreneur Frank Miller effectively lobbied the California state government to move the school to land he owned: forty acres on Magnolia Avenue in Riverside. Tourism was a motivating factor for Miller. He accurately presumed that Indian students would be a cheap source of labor and entertainment for his newly constructed Mission Inn, a luxurious resort.

Despite the outrage of the Perris community, Miller and Harwood Hall, superintendent of the Perris School, argued convincingly that an insufficient water supply made the Perris environment unhealthy for students, whereas Riverside had abundant water and a healthy, "civilizing" atmosphere—there had not been a "liquor saloon" in the city for many years. Their successful campaign resulted in congressional approval on May 31, 1901, of $75,000 for the construction of Sherman Institute. Hall was superintendent of Perris Indian School (which remained open for some students until 1904) from 1897 to 1904, of both schools from 1902 to 1904, and of Sherman Institute from 1902 to 1909. Hall had previously been superintendent of the Phoenix Indian School (a nonreservation school) and schools on the Quapaw (Oklahoma) and Pine Ridge (South Dakota) reservations.[2]

The cornerstone of the first building of Sherman Institute was laid on July 18, 1901, by A. C. Tanner, assistant commissioner of Indian Affairs. An autographed photo of James Schoolcraft Sherman, for whom the school was named, was included among the cornerstone artifacts. Sherman, U.S. congressman from 1886 to 1909, served as chairman of the Indian Affairs Committee and became vice president under William Howard Taft.[3]

The first student to register at Sherman Institute, on July 11, 1902, was Romaldo La Chusa, who was joined a few days later by eighteen other students from his Gila River Indian community in Sacaton, Arizona. He also was in the first graduating class in 1904. Speaking to a group of alumni in 1909, he said, "I am proud that I am an Indian, but I am prouder yet that you and I can become educated Indians. Education is all we need to make us strong and happy people. Sherman is our new mother. Let us always be glad that we came to Sherman. It has done much for us, and it will do more and more for our people."[4]

Even though financial support remained such a problem that when the first class graduated there were no funds for diplomas, La Chusa articulated his admiration for Harwood Hall's ambition that Sherman Institute be the epitome of successful federal Indian boarding schools. Silvas Lubo remembered, "In the early days it was necessary to advertise so people would know there was a Sherman Institute."[5] Hall and his successor, Frank M. Conser, superintendent from 1909 to 1931, cultivated a strong relationship between the school and the Riverside community.[6] Competitive sports were a surefire means of attracting public attention to Sherman Institute.

Hall and H. W. Mitchell, manager of the football team, arranged games with local high schools, out-of-state Indian schools, and colleges, including Stanford, the University of California at Berkeley, Occidental, Pomona, the University of Washington, and the University of Southern California. Sherman played USC from 1902 to 1906, winning every game. Hall successfully recruited Indian boys, using the competition with colleges as a selling point. To build on an already successful program, he also contracted with renowned coaches, including Cornell's football coach William J. Warner, brother of the celebrated "Pop" Warner, who coached at Carlisle Indian School during his illustrious career.[7]

Hall wrote on February 16, 1904, to Warner: "Your terms, $1200 and expenses, including transportation from Buffalo, for coaching football at this school for the four months ending January 1, 1905, are satisfactory and we will consider the matter as arranged. . . . I will place a fine lot of Indian material in your hands, for football, and we must beat Berkeley and Stanford this year if possible."[8] The amount of $1,200 for coaching four months, equal to about $30,000 in today's currency,[9] was generous considering the funding problems of federal Indian boarding schools. Hall evidently was relying on Sherman's share of gate receipts. In a letter dated February 18, 1904, to Ezra Decoto, manager of the USC football team, Hall suggested that the representatives of both teams "jointly manage the entire affairs [sic] so that no third party gets the lion's share of the receipts, as has been the custom in the past."[10]

A letter written on August 25, 1904, to Silvas Lubo is typical of Hall's recruiting: "Our coach, Mr. Warner, will be here within a day or so. Games have been arranged with Berkeley and Stanford. . . . Also have games arranged with Occidental, U.S.C. and Pomona. I hope you will be able to come September 1st and play with us this season. With a good team and a first class coach we ought to be the champions this year. . . . Of course, that depends on our showing. We can't get along without you, Faustino and Alex, and any other players you know of." The letter is signed, "Your Friend, Harwood Hall."[11]

The recruiting of Indian boys for football at the boarding schools had begun as early as 1899, when Richard Pratt wrote to the Sac and

Fox agent, "If you by chance have a sturdy young man anxious for an education who is swift of foot or qualified for athletics, send him and help Carlisle to compete with the great universities."[12] At the beginning of the twentieth century, the development of modern, overcrowded, socially unstable cities gave rise to the idea of sports as a wholesome activity that could condition and stabilize a diverse nation. Playgrounds and baseball fields were built in the middle of asphalt neighborhoods. The Progressive movement claimed that a healthy body was the manifestation of a healthy man, and "Muscular Christianity" became an axiom of the era.[13]

Football captured the American imagination; the annual Yale-Princeton game at the polo grounds in New York City drew crowds of 40,000 to 50,000. The excessive number of deaths and injuries caused by the game, however, resulted in a long and heated public debate. In 1904, twenty-one players were killed and more than two hundred injured. President Theodore Roosevelt, an ardent football fan, summoned representatives of Harvard, Yale, and Princeton to the White House on October 9, 1905, and commanded them to fix football.[14]

Following the national trend, as enthusiasm for football increased at Sherman, so did the risk for injury. Although most of the injuries from football were minor, some were fatal.[15] Football rule changes were made on the national level, most of them suggested by Pop Warner, and the game gradually became safer for the players.[16] It is a reasonable assumption that Jack Warner was aware of the changes in football suggested by his brother that were instituted to reduce the number of injuries.

During Conser's administration, the football program expanded, and football players were heroes. In addition to allowing Indian boys to show their prowess, the sport enabled them to travel to distant cities, to have special treatment in the dining hall, and to be awarded the powerfully symbolic team sweaters and coveted trophies that are still on exhibit in the Sherman Indian Museum. There is no documentation that Sherman demonstrated the extreme favoritism toward football players as did Carlisle when Pop Warner was coaching celebrated athletes, including Jim Thorpe. In 1907, an article in the *Chicago Sunday Tribune* accused Warner of ignoring athletes' drinking, cutting classes, and staying out after curfew.[17] A much milder criticism was voiced by a Kiowa student who attended Sherman in the 1920s who reported, "Even though I was academically way ahead of [football players,] they were looked up to."[18]

Other competitive sports, including baseball and long-distance running for boys and basketball for girls, also expanded, with Sherman students proving consistently victorious over their competitors.[19] Hopis regularly excelled in the running competitions. In December 1922, more than a thousand spectators watched the prize-winning Hopi boys in a cross-country race route throughout Riverside.[20]

As the public became more aware of Sherman Institute, the relationship between the Riverside community and the school grew stronger. Conser wrote in 1912, "The school is located in the midst of people of the highest culture and refinement, and the student of Sherman Institute is fortunate in his fight for character and education to be surrounded by such influences."[21] His remarks reflect the fundamental function of the school: the education and assimilation of Indian youths. Some historical documents claim that in the early years the school enrolled only so-called California Mission Indians, those who had been colonized by Spanish missionaries in the eighteenth and nineteenth centuries. Even though they had distinct indigenous names and cultures, the Indian Office used the term "Mission Indians" to refer to all Southern California Indians.[22] Students at the Perris School were all identified as Mission Indians from specific missions, but Sherman Institute in 1903 had enrolled students from the Gila River Reservation and a band of Akimel O'odham (Pima Indians), both from Arizona. In addition, Matthew Sakiestewa Gilbert in his study of Hopi Indians at Sherman Institute found one Hopi student enrolled in 1902 and another in 1903.

In 1906, seventy Hopi students were sent from their reservation in Orayvi (Oraibi), Arizona, to Sherman in a unique program. Unlike the first Hopis who entered Sherman, these students were not alone in coping with educational and cultural challenges. They were accompanied by their *kikmongwi* (chief), Tawaquaptewa, along with his wife, Nasumgoens, and daughter Mina, as well as other Hopi leaders. In *Education beyond the Mesas: Hopi Students at Sherman Institute, 1902–*

1929, Gilbert has admirably chronicled the history of this distinctive group. His work is the only study of a particular group of Indians at Sherman Institute; these Hopis exemplify the challenges facing Sherman Institute students in the first two decades of the school's history. Enrolled in classes designed for adults, the "elders in residence" learned very quickly. Tawaquaptewa learned English in less than five months and motivated his young followers to excel in all of their educational challenges. Despite a newspaper report that they were one of the most primitive tribes in the United States, these Hopi students outperformed other students in language acquisition and academic courses.[23]

By 1908, thirty-four buildings of the new campus had been completed and 550 students had been admitted. In 1909, forty-three tribes were represented, with students from California, the Southwest, the Pacific Northwest, and the plains. Sherman educated students in grades one to eight from 1902 to 1916. Although most students considered the eighth grade the completion of their education, grades nine and ten were added in 1916 for students who wished to continue. The eighth grade was the final grade for vocational instruction. During the early years at Sherman, the eight years of instruction were equivalent to six years in non-Indian schools.[24] Thomas Jefferson Morgan had explained the disparity by noting that federal Indian schools had the additional responsibilities of teaching English, introducing students to industrial training, and considerable attention to moral training.[25] By 1926, however, Sherman was offering complete elementary and high school curricula. Although in 1930–31 Sherman experienced its peak enrollment with 1,277 students, enrollment declined significantly from 1932 to 1945, during the Depression years.[26]

Following the models established by Morgan and Richard Henry Pratt, federal Indian boarding schools endeavored to "civilize" Indian children, an educational process that required the removal of the students from their Native languages and cultures. The curriculum of Sherman Institute was based on the ethnocentric belief in the superiority of white culture. As with all federal Indian boarding schools, a critical component of Sherman's education program was the insistence on the use of English only. If students were to be "civilized" and assimilated, the first task of educators was to teach them to read, write, and speak English. Indian students struggled with a language completely alien to the structures of their Native languages. When compelled to recite endless repetitions because of mistakes unknown to them, they trembled, cowed and humiliated.[27]

The insistence on English only was an assault on Indian children's identity. Learning English was not merely acquiring a new language; it meant that Indian children were thrust into new ways of thinking and of perceiving humanity and nature. Some Indian students resisted the eradication of their Native language and were successful. The Kiowas at Rainy Mountain Boarding School in Oklahoma, for example, mastered English and became bilingual, not relinquishing their Native language.[28] Supervisors Hall and Conser at Sherman Institute limited students' visits to their homes, convinced that these visits would cause students to revert to their Native languages and ways of life. Nevertheless, some Hopi children at Sherman returned home to the mesas no longer speaking Hopi, but being with their families allowed them to regain their Native language.[29]

Others strove to retain their Native language and failed. Viola Martinez, for one, was determined to speak her language at Sherman Institute: "I made up my mind I was not going to forget my language. I knew if I did, I would not be able to talk to my Aunt Mary Ann [who had raised her]. I remember they had tall palm trees at Sherman. . . . My cousin and I would climb up where we couldn't be seen or heard. . . . We wanted to talk Paiute so badly we would climb up in those trees." She was caught and punished repeatedly. She recalled, "I had to scrub the bathroom. This huge bathroom[:] . . . showers and bowls and toilet seats. Our matrons made us clean every inch." Eventually Viola did lose her language, a loss she grieved for the remainder of her life.[30]

In addition to English, reading, arithmetic, and U.S. history were taught in grades one through four. Because of the time required to master English, Indian students in a particular grade would be several years older than non-Indian students in the same grade. In the fifth grade, geography was added to the courses already being taught. In autobiographical accounts, edited by Michael C. Coleman, students expressed being astounded by geography. On being shown a globe of the earth, one reported being disoriented at the thought that his ancestors had roamed and hunted for untold ages on terrain that whirled around the sun. Another student claimed that geography had caused him to doubt his tribal learning, and he encountered adamant opposition when he attempted to educate his uncle regarding the Copernican theory. However, there were students who found geography fascinating when shown for the first time in their lives maps of Arizona. They located rivers and mountains they knew by their tribal names and some for which they knew the Spanish names. They took the geography book to the dormitory and almost "wore it out."[31]

Students had academic classes for half a day, with the remaining half devoted to vocational education. Not only did the history courses present the ethnocentric perspective of the superiority of white culture, but the textbooks portrayed Indians as barbarian obstacles to manifest destiny. Well into the twentieth century, the American education system was unreservedly slow in presenting the Indian experience with westward expansion, the displacement of Indian populations, and the exploitation of Indian resources. Instruction by both textbooks and teachers emphasized the superiority of white society.

The need for practical, vocational training in Indian education was given strong emphasis around the time Sherman Institute began admitting students. Vocational instruction—agriculture and industrial trades for the boys and domestic training for the girls—was designed to prepare students for economic self-sufficiency in white society. Because the Indian Office insisted that the schools be as self-sufficient as possible, the practical application of the vocational courses included manual labor for the maintenance of the school, growing and cooking their own food, making and mending their clothes, and cleaning and repairing the campus facilities.[32]

Most of the boarding schools maintained large-scale farms to provide fresh meat, fruit, vegetables, and dairy products to students and staff and also to provide training for the students. The Sherman Institute farm, 110 acres four miles south of the campus, consistently supplemented government commodities with fresh products. Sherman was a pioneer in developing irrigated pastures for dairy and beef cattle.[33]

Male and female students who worked on the farm, also called Sherman Ranch, lived on the property, supervised by instructors and dorm matrons. Their accommodation was constructed by boys, assisted by girls, with both groups consisting of students in the seventh to tenth grades. The cost of the entire construction was kept below $80 to demonstrate what could be done by families lacking the cash to purchase materials.[34] Salvaged lumber, old brick, rock, tree trunks, and palm leaves were used to keep building costs low.[35]

The work of the boys on the ranch included plowing, preparing the soil, raising stock, dairying, caring for horses, and blacksmithing. The girls did all the domestic work, as well as tending the poultry, milking cows, making butter, and canning fruits and vegetables. Katrina Paxton in her excellent study of gender in the education of Sherman students found that the girls were indoctrinated in the Protestant idea of "true womanhood." Women were expected to be, among other characteristics, pious, obedient, and meek. Paxton argues that in vocational training and in the classroom, Sherman fostered a significant transformation in the gender ideologies of female students.[36] Ironically, because the boys also were required to cook and bake, they occupied jobs that in Indian cultures were traditionally considered women's work.[37]

Partly because of the time required to acquire proficiency in English, vocational work overshadowed academic instruction and also reflected the government's goals of assimilation. Vocational instruction in the schools was expanded into the community in a program called "outing." Boys and girls who went "out" to live and work in homes, hotels, restaurants, and resorts, as well as on farms and ranches in the community, were learning how to be "civilized" and "useful."

The "outing" system was originally established by Richard Henry Pratt for the Carlisle school and had been an integral component of vocational education in Indian boarding schools since 1878. The system reflected the belief in the superiority of mainstream social order and the philanthropic, paternalistic attitude toward Indians. The Carlisle program was so successful that outing was expanded westward and by the beginning of the twentieth century was operative in several schools in the far west, including the Phoenix Indian School in Arizona.[38] The superintendent of the Phoenix school, who was exceptionally enthusiastic about the outing program, was Harwood Hall, who later became superintendent of the Perris Indian School, which had a well-established outing program, and Sherman Institute, where outing flourished under his administration.[39]

Boarding school supervisors became particularly committed to outing for girls. There was considerable demand for Indian girls who had been trained in domestic skills to work in homes doing cleaning, laundry, child care, and even cooking. At Sherman there was a continual demand for domestic work by girls.[40]

Founded in idealism at Carlisle, the outing system established at new locations deviated from its original purpose, and the schools came to be regarded as employment agencies, providing cheap labor to the community. Pratt was a vocal critic of outing as it was administered in the western schools even into his retirement years.[41]

David Wallace Adams describes Sherman boys sent out to ranches to harvest crops laboring "from daybreak to sunset in the hot sun" and sleeping in barns or tents, "never seeing the inside of a Victorian parlor, let alone being taken in as members of a middle-class family." He also points out, however, that the outing experience could be beneficial to students, giving them the opportunity to earn money and to explore the larger world.[42] Clara Moorhead, who attended Sherman from 1928 to 1932, reported leaving an outing job because the employer wanted her to learn gourmet cooking for parties and also because the man of the house was "peeking in the keyhole" of her room while she was resting. She liked that she was able to quit a job by simply calling the outing supervisors at Sherman, telling them that she did not like the job without giving reasons. She also liked being able to earn her own money. Viola Martinez, who attended Sherman during the same years as Clara, recalled the demoralizing outing experience of being unjustly accused of stealing a watch from her employer. However, she also related a significantly positive experience with an employer who told her she had a good mind: "She [the employer] encouraged me. I spent my evenings reading. That was the outing experience as I remember it. That is where I got the idea that I had a brain just like anybody else."[43]

Kevin Whalen, in his study of the outing system at Sherman Institute, illustrates other successful struggles through the middle course: "Many Sherman students entered the outing system on terms of their own choosing, and, once there, used the tools at hand to make the best of the situation."⁴⁴ Whalen asserts that although students in the outing system faced incredible challenges, his research shows that Sherman students were neither passive nor pliable, much less completely controlled by their employers.⁴⁵ "Like almost all aspects of federal Indian boarding schools in the early twentieth century, the outing system presented difficult and sometimes overwhelming challenges to young Native Americans. But . . . the young people at Sherman Institute demonstrated creativity and courage to draw from the outing system the most that they could."⁴⁶

Despite the positive experiences of some students, others used their outing experiences to run away from the boarding school. Sherman Institute's Outing Agent Fred Long recorded on October 24, 1928, that student Taft Coleta was a deserter from work on a theater building in Riverside. A notice was sent to law enforcement agencies throughout southern California: "Please apprehend and detain and call Sherman Institute." In the same year, Long recorded more than twenty-five deserters, both boys and girls, from outing jobs. Descriptions of these students included the word "digger," a derogatory term for California Indians, "half-breed" for one eleven-year-old boy, and others defined as "full-blood, half-degree, ¼ degree." One girl was described as having "black, beady eyes" and being "of the mulatto type."⁴⁷ Not only does the language of the outing agent reveal racist perceptions, but also the word "deserter" reflects the military regimen of Sherman Institute, an environment pervasive in all the federal Indian boarding schools.

Although the regimentation at Sherman was not as strict as in other boarding schools, military drills were used to teach order and discipline. Boys and girls were grouped according to age and size in military-style companies that marched to classes, to the dining room, and to the dorms. Max Mazzetti, president of the Sherman Alumni Association in 1992, described what he had learned about the military regimentation. There were regimental adjutants, majors, captains, lieutenants, sergeants, corporals, and privates. In the morning, they would march to raise the flag, march back to the dorm, clean their quarters, and march to the dining room for breakfast. In the evening, they would march with the band to the flagpole, receive the colors, and return to the dorm.⁴⁸ Military regimentation was particularly emphasized on Sundays when students in uniform, accompanied by the marching band, marched in a parade for the entertainment of visitors from the community.

The military regimen was one aspect of the moral training and code of conduct in which Sherman students were indoctrinated. Boys were given a printed *School Code: Governing the Conduct of the Boys*.[49] One of the purposes of the code was "to better familiarize boys with their duties." The code listed demerits and penalties for "acts of omission" and "acts of commission." Among the acts of omission were not wearing black shoes with their military uniforms, not wearing white gloves on inspection or regimental parade, not holding hat or cap on arm while marching in or out of chapel or dining room, neglecting to salute the officer of the day or an employee, and neglecting to tip the hat to the ladies. Acts of commission were more serious: being disobedient, using profanity, talking back to an officer or employee, visiting the girls' premises without permission, stealing, and becoming intoxicated or using tobacco in any form.

The code of conduct for girls was governed by the Victorian ideal of "true womanhood," with the attributes of piety, obedience, purity, and cleanliness. Katrina Paxton describes how the YWCA, which became an institutional fixture at Sherman Institute, influenced Sherman girls with lectures both on and off campus on the development of true womanhood and the importance of keeping themselves "sweet and attractive" at all times.[50]

As with other federal Indian boarding schools, the outing program at Sherman Institute was an extension of the domestic training in the classroom, preparing Sherman girls to be admirable domestics or wives. Paxton recounts the printed code of conduct, which was headed, "Outing Girls, Read Carefully."[51]

1. Never say you don't know how to do a task that you know but your employer wants done differently.
2. Adapt to [your] lady's way.
3. Keep your room clean and picked up.
4. Keep your door open to relieve odor.

The outing system had begun as early as 1893 at the Perris Indian School, which had a more comprehensive code of conduct, which was addressed to the "patron" and signed by Superintendent M. H.

Savage. Entitled "Rules to Govern Indian School Girls in Families," the rules were preceded by the statement, "Our objective in placing pupils in families is to advance them in English and in the customs of civilized life."

1. Do not allow the free use of money. Give spending money occasionally if asked for, but if it is spent for useless articles withhold it. When returning to the school send balance of wages due pupil to me.
2. Pupils must attend Sabbath School where such privileges are accessible.
3. Absence without permission must not be allowed, nor are girls to be out in the evenings, Saturday afternoons, public holidays or any pretense whatsoever, unless accompanied by some member of your family.
4. Pupils visiting their friends must not be encouraged to stay for meal. No girl can be allowed to receive visits from Indian or other young men without direct permission from the Superintendent of the school.
5. Frequent correspondence with other girls or boys must not be allowed, and writing or receiving of letters which girls are unwilling to show to patrons shall be just cause for ending such correspondence.
6. Patrons or others are not to hire pupils who have been sent to their neighbors without my consent, nor should students be encouraged to change places.
7. Except authorized by me, students are not to return or be returned to the school before the period for which they engaged expires.
8. Pupils must bath [sic] at least twice a week. Such clothing as needed by pupil can be provided out of earnings.
9. Encourage students to study and read off hours, even in busy seasons and give some assistance.
10. Explain monthly reports to pupils, have them sign them, and forward same to me.

The forms were to be signed by the superintendent, the patron, and the student, each retaining a copy.[52]

The students were a "captive audience" for white middle-class women intent on imparting not only the cult of true womanhood but also the Victorian ideology of "separate spheres." Superintendent Hall maintained separate spheres at Sherman with minimal contact between male and female students. Indeed, there was a demarcation line down the center of the campus, with boys walking on one side and girls on the other, no talking allowed. On bus trips, separation of the sexes was enforced by several chaperones.[53]

The *Sherman Bulletin*, the student publication, which was administered and edited by Sherman authorities, had a significant role in the enforcement of morals on campus. The publication included numerous adages advising students: Be truthful. Be faithful. Bad habits leave their mark. Keep silent about your troubles. Endure hardships; avoid brooding. The world owes you nothing. To their credit, administrators also printed student stories in virtually every issue, although each had a moral lesson. "The Red Coyote" was an admonishment against stealing. "How the Bear Lost His Tail" was a warning to be careful about what tricksters tell you. "The Chipmunk" had a straightforward message: listen to your elders. The *Sherman Bulletin* also listed the topics of religious lectures, which required student attendance; among them were "The Holy Name of Jesus," "Prayer," and "See King Jesus Early."[54]

Christianity had been an integral component of Indian education since the beginning; conversion to Christianity by Indians was essential to their becoming "civilized." Whereas religious instruction was presented in the classroom by most Indian boarding schools, Sherman Institute did not offer courses on the Bible or theology during the first four decades of its history. However, Bible study, chapel services, and attendance at religious lectures were required of the students. The resolute goal of converting Indian students to Christianity was rarely completely successful. While students may have accepted various Christian beliefs, many retained their own spiritual values, blending tribal and white traditions.[55]

A poignant expression of Christian dominance, however, is the Sherman cemetery, located in the area that was once the school farm. In 1944, the Department of the Interior sold the farm acreage except for the half-acre cemetery, where sixty-seven children were buried between 1904 and 1955, far from their homes and their spiritual beliefs. School officials administered Christian funeral services.[56] After several years of neglect, a plaque was installed in 1974 by the Native Daughters of the Golden West in memory of these children, and local tribes initiated an annual Flower Day in May, during which the graves are groomed and decorated.[57]

Several of the children buried in the cemetery had died of typhoid fever. A devastating typhoid epidemic in 1904 had infected forty-two children, seven of whom died.[58] Others had died from tuberculosis, which resulted in more student deaths than any other single disease.[59] However, Jean Keller in *Empty Beds: Indian Student Health at Sherman Institute, 1902–1922* concludes that Sherman students had relatively good health due to several factors. First, the Indian Office was prioritizing health issues, enacting preventive health policies. Second, Superintendents Harwood Hall and Frank Conser were effective advocates of good student health. In addition, Sherman was located in a temperate climate and had a supportive community, abundant water, and productive farmland.[60]

Although illness was exacerbated by inadequate diet in many of the boarding schools, Sherman Institute was fortunate in that its farm provided fresh fruit and vegetables and dairy products.[61] Despite these positive factors, Matthew Sakiestewa Gilbert records the deaths from tuberculosis of Hopi students in 1908 and 1919.[62] Sherman alum Viola Martinez remembered that in the late 1920s there was a lot of illness in the school: "It seemed to me there were always real sick children in the hospital." She also remembered hearing from Indian people that they expected children sent to Sherman to "come back dead." The only time Viola went home, she escorted her cousin "in a casket to the reservation."[63]

The hospital to which Viola refers was constructed on campus in 1909 during Conser's administration, only four years after Superintendent Hall had Sherman's first hospital built. Both construction projects were remarkable in light of persistent limited funding. As Keller points out, 1909 was a significant year for forceful action by the Indian Office, under the supervision of Commissioner Francis E. Leupp and his successor, Robert G. Valentine, to prevent the increasing disease and death rates in the boarding schools. Superintendents used health as a reason for funding requests, arguing that every facility had a beneficial effect in preventing disease. Hall and Conser lobbied resolutely for this funding.⁶⁴ In 1905 Hall had received a letter from C. Fairlane, acting commissioner of the Office of Indian Affairs, questioning his request for the authority to spend $496 for employees' reception rooms, pupils' quarters, and a special cooking department, because the costs appeared "rather high."⁶⁵

Additionally, Hall and Conser both were advocates of fresh air to help students maintain good health, but it was not until Conser became superintendent that physical exercise became an essential means of preventing illness.⁶⁶ Although since its opening in 1902 Sherman had always had large playing fields, these were intended for competitive sports. Hall was a great enthusiast of Sherman's sports programs, but he considered these solely as means for gaining community support for the school. During Conser's twenty-two-year administration, competitive sports remained privileged and admired, but he was determined that outdoor physical activities become an essential factor in the daily life of all Sherman students.⁶⁷

In 1909, at the beginning of Conser's administration, Commissioner Leupp resolved that off-reservation boarding schools should be less regimented. Although Leupp was not able to implement his resolution, his successor, Robert Valentine, urged that the schools set up playgrounds for their students, and in 1913 the Indian Office mandated playgrounds on every nonreservation boarding school campus.⁶⁸ Unlike many other supervisors, Conser accepted the mandate with enthusiasm and created separate playgrounds for boys and girls that were used daily for outdoor sports and free play.⁶⁹ The Hopi students, in particular, did not simply excel in baseball, football, basketball, and distance running; they remembered their culture and taught indigenous Hopi games to non-Hopi students. The Hopis and other Indian students in the boarding schools were indoctrinated in the ideal of winning, not showing respect for opponents but consistently defeating them.⁷⁰

Military drills had been an essential function of the daily "exercise" routine since the opening of Sherman Institute. Essential to the drills were the marching bands. Sherman band members practiced for an hour every evening and performed at football games, Sunday roll call, and concerts on campus and parades in the community. Indian school marching bands went farther afield, too, even to world's fairs: the band of Carlisle played at the Chicago World's Columbian Exposition as early as 1893, and the band of Sherman Institute performed at the San Francisco Panama-Pacific International Exposition in 1915.[71]

Despite the military regimentation, Sherman offered a wide range of extracurricular activities. In addition to the foremost diversion of sports, students enjoyed movies, dances, ping-pong, speech contests, and music. Although these activities were recreational, many of them were designed to promote the superiority of white culture. A universal aspect of the assimilation efforts in the boarding schools was "American" music, which pervaded boarding school campuses. Students were taught to play the piano and woodwind, brass, and string instruments. Many of the boarding schools, including Sherman, had integrated choirs in which boys and girls learned patriotic and Christian songs in English. These songs, "safer" than the "heathen" pleasures of their Native music, were performed for white visitors to the school and for civic groups in nearby towns. Their music celebrated American patriotism and reinforced Anglo-European social and artistic values in an attempt to eradicate Native expressions of creativity. Having been raised in cultures that valued music, Indian students welcomed learning new instruments and compositions. Those at Sherman formed a variety of music clubs, which created especially bright moments in their regimented days. Indeed, music was so important to a fifteen-year-old Sioux girl that in 1925 she left Sherman because she was not allowed to play her mandolin in the club.[72]

As with other assimilation strategies, the effort to "civilize" Indian students through music was not completely successful. While students were learning Bach and Beethoven, they were also discovering the music forms of their peers from reservations nationwide and incorporating them into their own indigenous style.[73] Many students introduced the music they had been taught in boarding school to their Native communities, where it was adapted for their Indigenous musical expression. Frank David Blackhoop (Wind on the Forehead), a Standing Rock Lakota, graduated from Hampton Institute in 1922, using his musical education in several teaching positions in Indian schools, while composing Indian tribal melodies and lecturing throughout the nation on Indians and their music. He completed his career at Sherman Institute in 1935.[74]

The Hopis had a particularly rewarding experience with music at Sherman. While they were becoming skilled at American and European music, their leader, Tawaquaptewa, was also effective in having students demonstrate Hopi music and dance both on and off campus. In teaching them to perform the Eagle Dance, he set a precedent for Hopi music at Sherman that continues to the present. The students also instructed each other in Hopi songs and stories, preserving, as Matthew Sakiestewa Gilbert states, "the Hopi way through an institution designed to destroy it."[75]

The integration of Native and white culture was not always achieved by boarding school students. Not surprisingly, scholars have found that many ex-students learned that the knowledge acquired in the boarding school was irrelevant on the reservation, while others expressed their belief that their education did help them in later life in their traditional communities. Many students upon returning home became intermediaries between white and Indian societies, a necessary but problematic responsibility.[76]

Some of the encounters between former students and their parents were painful. When Polingaysi Qoyawayma, after graduating from Sherman Institute, returned to New Orayvi, Arizona, the poverty of the scene made her heartsick. When her mother showed her beautiful plaques she had made for Polingaysi's wedding, the image of herself as a traditional Hopi bride was appalling: "This life was not for her. She had gone too far along the path of the white man."[77] Similarly, Viola Martinez cried when she reported that when she returned to the reservation in Owens Valley, California, Aunt Mary Ann, who had raised her, did not recognize her, and because Viola was unable to speak Paiute, she could not communicate with her aunt. She remembered, "I was unfamiliar with the customs and traditions of my people and unacceptable because of my Anglo-oriented education and training."[78]

Demonstrating remarkable effort and persistence, both Polingaysi Qoyawayma and Viola Martinez eventually did reconnect with their cultures in ways that were of significant value to their communities. Both became teachers: Qoyawayma in Indian schools and Martinez in Los Angeles. Qoyawayma battled opposition from both the Indian and white communities to educate Indian students "from what they already know, not from a totally new, strange field of experience." After three decades of teaching young Indian children, she became an advocate for higher education for Hopis, establishing a scholarship fund for students who wanted to continue but could not finance their education.[79]

Viola Martinez, who taught in the Los Angeles Unified School District from 1968 to 1984, was a founding member of the Los Angeles American Indian Education Commission. One of the priorities of the commission was to educate non-Indians about Indian people. The respect and affection shown Viola by young Indian people are testimony to the fact that her experiences at Sherman Institute have enabled her to counsel them with a sensitivity born of firsthand experience.[80]

The severe challenges that returning students encountered were the result of the intent of their boarding school education to Christianize and "civilize" them. Moreover, as Commissioner Leupp complained, students in boarding schools were maturing in an environment they would never see duplicated at home, which created a disdain for life on their reservations.[81] In 1917, Commissioner Cato Sells declared that Indian students whose parents could afford their education or those who lived near public schools should be removed from federal boarding schools. His policy led in 1920 to the closing of twelve boarding schools with low enrollment, Sherman Institute not being one of them.[82]

Nearly nine thousand American Indians served in the armed forces during World War I and were subsequently granted citizenship. In 1924, the Indian Citizenship Act, also known as the Snyder Act, granted U.S. citizenship to Indians with the support of white activists who hoped to empower Indians through citizenship.[83] Despite these progressive actions, the federal government during the first half of the decade of the 1920s resolutely resisted change in its Indian education policy. Mounting criticism by white activists forced the federal government to rethink Indian education policy, however. Predominant among the reformers was John Collier, a Progressive who founded the American Indian Defense Association in 1923. The relentless campaigns of Collier and other reformers against the ethnocentric Indian policy led to a comprehensive evaluation of Indian affairs authorized in 1926 by Hubert Work, secretary of the Interior.

Conducted by the Institute for Government Research, and to avoid bias, it was financed by the Rockefeller Foundation. In 1928 the survey team, directed by Lewis Meriam, issued an 848-page report entitled *The Problem of Indian Administration*, which became referred to as the

Meriam Report. The prevailing argument of the education section of the report, written by W. Carson Ryan, Jr., was that the most fundamental need in Indian education was a change in point of view.[84] The report strongly criticized the policy of removing Indian children from their home environment. It further asserted that without recognizing the diversity among Indian tribes and the uniqueness of each Indian student, education methods would be "worse than futile" (346). Cultural aspects of Indian life should be incorporated into the education program (351), and uprooting children from their natural environment, forcing them to accept white values, then returning them to their Native environs was to "invite disaster" (407).

The most severe criticisms were related to "deplorable health conditions" (392) and the labor of children in Indian boarding schools, which was denounced as "a violation of child labor laws" (376). The Meriam Report did find that Sherman Institute students were the best-fed of all the government boarding school children, partly because the students worked hard on the school farm to produce fresh produce and dairy products. Nevertheless, their diet was inadequate, because the government expenditure for each student was just eighteen cents per day.[85]

An especially compelling criticism was directed at a program in which children as young as eleven years were being sent, as part of their vocational education, to beet fields in Colorado and Kansas. The official brochure issued by the Phoenix office of the Indian Service described the work as light, although tedious, with the best thinning of the beets being done "stooping over or on hands and knees." The brochure stated, "Small boys are very well adapted to this work."[86]

The Meriam Report reveals that the boys had to pay part of their earnings, which were not specified, to their foreman and their cook. They were also charged one dollar a season for the hoes they used in thinning the beets, a dollar a month for "hospital," and twenty dollars a month for transportation to and from the beet fields in government trucks.[87] The report stresses the dangers of placing work assignments for students "in the hands of persons who, however excellent their intentions, have so little conception of the right relation between education and industry" (391).

Ryan, who later served as the BIA director of education (1930–33), systematically examined and criticized all phases of Indian education. In addition to student health and labor, he investigated funding, administrative and teaching personnel, the curriculum, discipline, military regimentation, maintenance of the schools, religious indoctrination, and the outing system.

The publication of the report coincided with the Progressive antiassimilation movement, and John Collier and other activists campaigned to close the boarding schools. Although between 1928 and 1933 twelve schools were either closed or converted to day schools, enrollments were soaring. During the Great Depression, the public schools were facing financial crisis, and in 1933 the Office of Indian Affairs sent letters to boarding schools advising them to admit only the neediest children because families were asking to send children to the schools in unprecedented numbers.[88] Poverty conditions forced even the most conservative Indians to send their children to federal boarding schools, which were already underfunded. Funding was decreased even more because of the prevailing economic circumstances. Sherman Institute had its peak student population of 1,277 in 1930–31 and became an accredited high school in 1932, but unlike what occurred with other boarding schools, its enrollment declined during the subsequent Depression years.[89]

The Great Depression created considerable doubt about the direction of the country, and the Meriam Report validated the need for major change in the Indian affairs policy of the federal government. The report was a crucial influence on all aspects of the policy, laying a foundation for the reforms made by John Collier during his tenure as commissioner of Indian Affairs, from 1933 to 1945.

Perris Indian School, Perris, California, 1900.

Sherman Institute building at the Magnolia Avenue site, constructed in 1901.

One of the four dormitories constructed by 1908 on the Sherman Institute's Riverside campus.

The Ramona Building, a dormitory for older boys, circa 1960.

Romaldo La Chusa, member of the first graduating class. The photograph's caption states "first Sherman graduate 1903," but the first graduating class was 1904.

Class of 1904, Perris Indian School.

Grade school girls at Perris Indian School, 1908.

Grade school boys at Perris Indian School, 1908.

Girls on the Sherman Institute's Riverside campus, early twentieth century.

Sherman Indian Museum (on left), the only original building of the school, situated in the attractive landscaping of the campus.

Sherman Indian High School campus in 2013, designed to meet the twenty-first-century needs of Indian students.

Sherman Indian High School's restructured and modernized eighty-eight-acre campus in 2013.

2

Reform, War, and Innovation

1934-1952

FRANKLIN D. ROOSEVELT, ELECTED PRESIDENT in 1932 with a mandate for reform, appointed Harold Ickes secretary of the Interior. John Collier, who had introduced Ickes to the critical challenges in Indian affairs, was named commissioner of Indian Affairs.[1] His tenure (1933–45) became known as the Indian New Deal, during which Progressive education and anthropology provided the framework for Indian education. Collier and Willard Beatty, the director of the Education Division of the BIA, were convinced that Indian education should originate in the Native community and emphasize traditional values and culture.[2] Beatty visited Sherman in 1936, proclaiming in several speeches that the assimilationist policy was not working: "Educating students away from their tribe under conditions destructive to social controls had not proved successful." He also noted that the Depression had least affected farmers and Sherman should provide more training in land use.[3]

Two statutes enacted in 1934 were milestones for Indian education: the Indian Reorganization Act and the Johnson-O'Malley Act. The Indian Reorganization Act (IRA) provided a measure of self-determination for Indians in education and also in religion, land allotments, and tribal government.[4] The new anti-assimilation policy introduced innovative tenets in education: children, while becoming aware of white values and culture, would be taught primarily from the perspective of their Native cultures; Indian Service instructors would be sensitive to Indian cultures and provide lessons appropriate to the characteristics and needs of Indian children; military regimentation would be eliminated; vocational education would teach skills appropriate for work in

Native communities; and there would be no interference with Indian religious or ceremonial expressions.[5] Partly in response to the move by the federal government toward self-determination, Sherman Institute students formed a student council in 1938 that soon developed into an intertribal council.[6]

The Johnson-O'Malley Act authorized the federal government to pay states for educating Indians in public schools. As with the IRA, the Johnson-O'Malley Act also provided assistance in areas other than education: medical, agricultural, and social welfare. This assistance was in response to findings that Indians needed support in their transition from Indian-only to general-population environments. The problems of federal-state relationships were myriad.[7] Nevertheless, it was the first legislation to provide federal funds for Indian children in public schools. The effectiveness of the act is evident in the fact that all BIA high schools became accredited during the 1940s.[8]

Despite the significant positive changes of the Indian New Deal, the labor of Indian children had continued to be necessary to support boarding schools during the financial burden of the 1930s. Sherman students were engaged in courses in farming, dairy and livestock husbandry, electric shop, plumbing, engineering, auto mechanics, masonry, mill cabinetry, mineralogy, printing, shoe repair, tailoring, sewing, cosmetology, laundry, kitchen work, and baking, all of which could be used to maintain the school and some of which could be marketed to the community. An additional source of income was derived from an Indian arts and crafts course to prepare Sherman boys to teach summer campers how to make imitation Indian pottery, basketry, and blankets using burlap.[9] Not only was this practice ironic, it ignored the cultural meanings of Native arts and crafts. Sherman was exploiting students, teaching them to imitate their culture to support the school financially.

A New Deal Agency, the National Youth Administration (NYA), focused on providing work and education for Americans between the ages of sixteen and twenty-five. The program was in effect from 1935 to 1939 as part of the Works Progress Administration (WPA). Approximately 475,000 boys and girls were paid for "work study" projects.[10] Evidence that NYA students attended Sherman is provided in an article in 1937 in the *Sherman Bulletin*, titled "NYA Students at Sherman, ½ and ½ days." The unnamed author states, "Only through such projects will boys of stricken families avail themselves of better jobs in their communities and a higher standard of living." NYA students were enrolled in an arrangement of courses familiar to Sherman, a half day each of study and work.[11]

Further involvement of Sherman with the WPA can be seen in cleaning and construction work on campus. In 1938, WPA workers, assisted by Sherman students, charted the grounds, creating a map of the campus, and cleaned and renovated the walls, ceilings, windows, floors, and drapes of all the buildings.[12] In 1939 a job costing $18,000 was funded by the Department of the Interior for one hundred workers to renovate roadways, walks, curbs, and gutters and to pave the parade ground so students could have an area on which to roller skate and have outdoor dances.[13] A $25,000 joint investment by the WPA and the Indian Service in 1939 provided the Sherman campus with new sidewalks, pavements, and curbs.[14] Also in 1939, trees were removed and 150 new ones were planted on the campus. The WPA workers were assisted by Sherman boys, operating skiploaders, conveyers, trucks, and tractors and maintaining the equipment.[15]

During the late 1930s, there evidently was concern among Sherman's students about the possibility of the United States engaging in war. A column in the *Sherman Bulletin* on Armistice Day in 1939 argued, "We see no reason why our country should be involved in another war. The last war taught us that we have absolutely nothing to gain if we were to enter again. We are certain that we lost more friends than we gained. Above all else we know that each American will do all in his or her power to keep the country out of the war."[16]

Despite this sentiment, Sherman Institute found itself involved in virtually every phase of World War II. Sherman had its first blackout on December 9, 1941. Superintendent Donald H. Biery complimented the students and staff on their efficient blackout preparations. Parents had expressed fear for the safety of their children. Biery repeatedly emphasized that there was "no immediate danger," only commonsense precautionary measures on the assumption that it was better to be well prepared for a possible emergency. In keeping with these precautions, certain rooms in the dorms and the gym and auditorium were to have darkened windows.[17]

In a message one year later, Biery conveyed additional war-related news that may not have been welcomed by parents:[18]

> The leaders of our country have asked all of us, including children, to do our part in assisting the war effort by working, studying, reducing vacations and stopping needless travel. Sherman is endeavoring to do its part by not having a Christmas vacation this year, but instead will conduct school through Christmas week. The students will go right on with their classes on every week day, except for Christmas Day.
>
> Since travel by train and bus is now reserved for soldiers and sailors during the Holidays, we strongly advise against children trying to travel during this time since they may be stranded in a city for several days waiting a chance to obtain a seat. We cannot be responsible for the welfare of students who attempt to travel during this rush season. Girls in particular are in danger of being led into trouble by unscrupulous persons.
>
> Your child will be well cared for at Sherman. . . . [M]any recreational activities have been planned, including a special New Year's Eve dance. So if your child asks to come home for Christmas we suggest that you instruct him or her to remain.
>
> Wishing you a Merry Christmas and a Happy New Year,
>
> Sincerely yours, D. H. Biery. Supt.

Sherman Institute contributed to the war effort in myriad ways. In addition to the more than three hundred men and women who were current and former students and employees serving in the armed forces, Sherman had contributed 145,554 tons of scrap metal and rubber by the end of 1942.[19] No information is available as to where Sherman obtained such a hefty amount of metal and rubber. On a lesser level, no new light bulb was issued in the school unless the burned-out or broken one was returned in exchange.[20]

In March 1943 Sherman was given high praise by Clay Freeman, chairman of the Riverside Defense Council, for the "efficient manner in which a simulated bombing attack was carried out during the night."

With the entire student body participating, a dozen "casualties" from high explosives and incendiaries were reported. The hospital was ready to take care of them. More than two hundred students were "evacuated" from a dorm. The kitchen was open and staffed to feed between three hundred and four hundred persons. Students equipped with shovels and axes traveled by bus to the site of the "bombing" at Magnolia and Van Buren Avenues to clear the highway for military vehicles. An official of Riverside Defense Council who witnessed the test stated that the students and staff of Sherman Institute had proven that they would be ready "at a moment's notice if an enemy invasion threatened."[21]

Funding for off-reservation boarding schools was further constricted during World War II, and the military drafting of male students caused extra burdens for the female students, who assumed responsibility for much of the work on the ranch and dairy, as well as the hard work in the kitchen that was required for preparing meals in large, heavy quantities. The shortage of labor was made worse in November 1940 by a flu epidemic that sent eighty-nine students to the hospital and confined thirty-three additional sick students to the Tepee and Minnehaha dorms.[22]

Meanwhile, female students were taking the Rural Home Life course, which involved living on the ranch as a family of limited income would, taking care of poultry, rabbits, and livestock, preparing meals, caring for children, sewing, and furnishing the cottage cheaply. They cleaned the ranch property with hoes, shovels, and picks, then planted a large garden with vegetables and flowers. To augment the income of the "family of limited means," they sold eggs and vegetables.[23] In March 1943, a large section of the farm was leased to a private individual for three years with a revocable permit. The leasing of the property was necessitated by insufficient labor to manage the farm.[24]

The war had a dramatic effect on the population and vocational education of Sherman Institute. In December 1941, in particular, Beatty wrote a memo to Biery, calling attention to the fact that Sherman was located in the center of an active industrial development in defense production: "We believe that every effort should be made to use Sherman facilities to the maximum." Referring to the demand for skilled craftsmen such as Sherman students trained in metalwork, Beatty proposed that the school accept older students interested in securing jobs in the defense industry.[25]

Sherman administrators and faculty agreed to the proposal and enrolled older students, who paid a monthly tuition of $15.[26]

Defense industries, including Solar Aircraft and Vegas Aircraft corporations, persuaded Superintendent Biery to permit Indian girls to enroll in classes in defense training. Especially persuasive were arguments such as "Airplane factories are hiring women and expect to hire more as the war progresses. Sherman is favorably located and equipped to give training to girls who have the ability to profit by the training." Sherman Institute also received permission from the Office of Indian Education to enroll in its defense training program adult Indians between the ages of twenty and thirty-five who were not subject to Selective Service.[27]

Aircraft welding, previously taught at Sherman exclusively to Indians, was made available to white students because of the critical need for skilled welders in the defense industry. Job placement was guaranteed after a training period of two months. Women welders were preferred because of the Selective Service prospects for men. Intensive training offered to men and women included electric welding, gas welding, machine shop, auto mechanics, and wood shop. All students who had completed a course of training at Sherman were employed in defense work.[28]

Although more than three hundred employees and current and former students from Sherman enlisted in the armed forces, some Indian groups did not understand the Selective Service and refused to register. Others refused on religious grounds, because of fear of discrimination, or because they considered the draft a violation of their rights granted in treaties with the federal government. Indeed, one small group of Tohono O'odham (Papago) refused to register, claiming that they thought they were not a part of the United States. In contrast, the Crow nation donated $10,000 to the federal government for ammunition, and the Oregon Klamaths invested $150,000 to build a trade school to train skilled workers for shipyards and airplane factories.[29]

During the postwar administration of President Harry S. Truman (1945–53) and Commissioner William A. Brophy (1945–48), the policy was a dramatic swing back to assimilation. Federal Indian policy regressed even further during the years Dillon S. Myer was commissioner (1950–53). The movement toward assimilation had been furthered by more than twenty-four thousand Indians serving in the armed forces. Among the most well-known are the Navajo code talkers. Not as well-known are the Hopi code talkers. LeRoy Shingoitewa has said, "These Hopi men were humble and did not talk about what they did in combat."[30]

Thousands of Indians who were too old for military service engaged in defense work in cities. At the end of World War II, Indian men and women who had been in military service and those who had been employed in the defense industry returned to the reservations and extolled the value of an education to prepare Indians to function successfully in mainstream society. The Indian education policy was then designed to train students for jobs in the growing metropolitan areas.[31]

The most significant program created by this policy was the Navajo Special Education Program. (Because the documents concerning this special education program refer to the students as Navajo, this term will be used here rather than the traditional Diné.) Although the need for postwar employment was critical for Navajos, the educational system on the Navajo Reservation was critically underfunded and underdeveloped, with only 32 percent of Navajo children enrolled.[32] The federal government responded to this need with one of the most innovative programs ever devised by the Bureau of Indian Affairs. L. Madison Coombs, educational specialist for the Bureau of Indian Affairs, expressed the philosophy of the program: "Navajo children each had but one life to live and youth was fleeting. Delay would condemn them to a life of ignorance, illiteracy and inadequacy in a modern world."[33] The remedy was the creation of the Navajo Special Education Program—five years of concentrated study and work, designed to provide Navajo adolescents with a vocational skill and sufficient fluency in English to guarantee off-reservation jobs.

The federal government selected Sherman Institute for the pilot program, which was described as experimental, since there were no experiential guidelines.[34] During the first three years, the major goals were basic skills in English and math and social and personal development in conforming to white society. During the fourth and fifth years, the emphasis was on the acquisition of marketable vocational skills.

In October 1946, Sherman enrolled 290 Navajos ages twelve to twenty who had never experienced formal education.[35] The federal government employed the Santa Fe railroad to transport the students from Arizona to Riverside, California. Most of the students had never traveled beyond their reservation, and few of them had even seen a train.

The Navajo Program depended on distinct features not available in regular boarding school programs: a short-range curriculum with definite goals, directors and teachers among the best in the Indian Service and assisted by Navajo interpreters, and, in theory, at least, adequate funding. The first objective of the program was daunting: the students would complete three years' work in 180 days. This challenge was intensified by the fact that most of the Navajo students were not literate in their Native language.

Despite this intimidating expectation, the pilot program at Sherman Institute was deemed successful at the end of the first year. In the fall of 1947, the Navajo Program was resumed at Sherman, and in 1948 the regular elementary and high school programs were discontinued and no California Indians were permitted at the school. In the fall of 1949, the progress of the beginners justified the belief in their ability to complete the basic courses in six months.[36]

The Navajo Program was also established in 1947–48 at three additional schools: Chilocco Indian School in Oklahoma, Phoenix Indian School in Arizona, and Carson Indian School (renamed Stewart Indian School) in Nevada. In 1948–49, Navajo Special Education Programs were opened in Albuquerque Indian School in New Mexico, Chemawa Indian School in Oregon, and the Cheyenne-Arapaho School in Oklahoma. From the fall of 1947 to the spring of 1949, the Special Navajo Education Program had grown from 290 students in one school to 1,650 students in seven schools. In 1951 Sherman graduated 101 students in the first class of the program.[37] Although the program was still called the Navajo Special Education Program, ninety-eight Tohono O'odham youths and fifteen Apaches were enrolled at Sherman in 1949.[38] In 1950, Congress further expanded the program with passage of the Navajo-Hopi Long-Range Rehabilitation Act (PL 81-474) to construct basic facilities on the Navajo and Hopi reservations, including the building of schools.[39]

The Sherman program emphasized two key elements: the students were not to be expected to be something they weren't, and Native culture was not to be demeaned. These elements illustrate the well-meaning intention of the creators and administrators of the program, and the students' cultures were respected in the employment of Native language interpreters. However, a transcript of an orientation session at Sherman given by Cleora C. Helbing as late as 1951 reveals a gap between intention and practice that reveals the persistence of a deep-seated ethnocentrism:

> Your people, your fathers and mothers have sent you here determined that you learn the ways of the White man. You will learn to talk like the White man. You will learn to speak English. You will learn the White man's songs. You will learn to dress like the White man. You will learn to behave like the White man. You will learn to eat the same food as the White man. . . . Now I would like to talk to you about taking food on your tray. I am going to shock you. The first meal that you had here, you wasted between $50.00 and $78.00 worth of food. You will be working all of your life to earn enough money to buy food. I have been on the Navajo, Papago and Apache reservations. I do not have to tell any of you that there is not enough food on the reservation to make you strong. It is not right to waste food. That is a bad habit. When you have good habits you will eat everything on your tray.[40]

Although Helbing is confronting the reality of what the students will learn at Sherman, the aggressive tone she uses is a negative reinforcement of white superiority. Her lecture is an obvious violation of the principle of respecting Native culture and student individuality.

Despite the ultimate success of the pilot project, Sherman's Navajo Special Education Program had considerable difficulty during the first few years. Paramount was the necessity of pairing Native language interpreters with the teachers. World War II military veterans were especially effective as interpreters, but while their experience in the major culture and their command of English were impressive, these attributes were not comprehensive. The interpreters had to do their own homework, studying the material to be presented. Many words and concepts in English had no direct equivalents in the Native languages. Although the students were mature and intelligent enough to understand the material in their Native language, presenting too many new ideas or words in English would confuse them and obstruct learning.[41] Despite these formidable difficulties in acquiring English, the Navajo students eventually wrote and printed the student newspaper, the *Sherman Bulletin*, for twelve years, sending it to nine off-reservation boarding schools and day schools on reservations.[42]

The difficulty of the mission of the Navajo Program was intensified by the lack of appropriate educational materials. The English skills of the students were comparable to those of a non-Native five-year-old, but they were adolescents and resented being required to read texts that treated them like "babies." The instructional staff had unsatisfactory results in their attempts to simplify more difficult published material, and as the students progressed in the program, they required more complex content. Ultimately, in 1951 the Bureau of Indian Affairs employed a former Indian Service teacher and published author, who successfully revised the texts of the entire curriculum.[43]

Difficulties in the instructional program were also worsened by inadequate and poorly prepared staff. In 1948 Norma C. Runyan, supervisor of Indian education, reported to Willard W. Beatty, director of education for the Bureau of Indian Affairs, that there was "a significant need for more teacher-interpreters," but Sherman's "tight budget" forced her to recommend getting along as best as they could. Observing that some of the teachers were not "adjusting too happily to the work," she believed that the difficult adjustment was due to "an unexpressed feeling that the present type of program is temporary and the good old days will return." Mythus Evans, superintendent of Sherman Institute, assured her that eventually the situation would "straighten out."[44]

A major contribution of the interpreters was their understanding of beliefs, values, and customs of the students' Native cultures. Helping students develop social skills appropriate to white society became a primary responsibility of the interpreters. Before coming to Sherman, many of the students had never slept in a bed, eaten with silverware, or used bathtubs, showers, or flush toilets. Washing and ironing clothes, shining shoes, and maintaining order and cleanliness in dorm rooms required learning how to use unfamiliar laundry equipment, vacuum cleaners, floor wax, furniture polish, and window cleaners.[45]

There was also a persistent problem in the boys' grooming and the care of their dormitory at Sherman. Runyan reported, "The boys' appearance has been especially poor at this school. . . . It is the weakest spot now in the entire school." She attributed this problem to the lack of leadership of the boys' adviser, whose qualifications she questioned. The girls, in contrast, were described as taking great pride in their grooming to the extent that they "took advantage of [hair] permanents given at the school of cosmetology in Riverside."[46]

Some of the instruction required of both teachers and interpreters was both less tangible and more significant than advice on grooming. Students had to learn, for example, a completely different way of thinking about property. Because piñon trees on the Navajo Reservation were owned in common by the community and not considered the property of a particular individual, Navajo boys seeing ripe dates lying under the trees in an orchard helped themselves. The angry owner complained to school authorities that the boys had stolen his dates. The boys responded that the dates were under a tree, not in the man's house.[47] The question arises: since they were not on the Navajo Reservation, did the boys perhaps know that what they were doing was wrong?

A problem unique to the structure of the Navajo Program was that of students who had been admitted when they were "quite old." Students who were older than twenty were allowed to skip one or more years of the basic curriculum before beginning vocational instruction. These students were unable to progress as well as students who had completed the basic courses and were unhappily aware of their deficiency. The Sherman staff concluded that placing a student ahead of his actual achievement because he was older was not good policy. It was considered a worthwhile experiment, however, and the policy was not discarded completely but was employed with extreme care, assessing students individually upon admission, rather than assigning them by age.[48]

Not all of the unsuccessful episodes of the program were deemed worthwhile experiments. In 1948, Runyan wrote with obvious dismay about an instructor who was supposed to be teaching girls how to clean hallways but instead was working with the sweeper herself. When questioned, she responded, "That's what I am, a maid." The girls involved were most likely expressing resistance by either refusing to clean the hallways or pretending they did not know how. Clearly disturbed, Runyan reported, "I agree with Mr. Evans that much of this undercurrent which breaks out on the surface . . . will run its course and subside, but these people should be given guidance."[49]

By 1950, however, Runyan's report revealed Evans's prediction to be correct: "Sherman has gone through four years in which the work was new to many people, and everyone wondered how it would really come out. This year the whole group appears to feel more secure in the work they are doing, and the quality of the work in the majority of departments is good." More significantly, she observed that "the general morale of the total group at Sherman" was very high.[50]

Regardless of the improved morale, not every student stayed in the program, and although the numbers were small, dropouts were inevitable. Of the 290 students at Sherman during the first year, only 5 dropped out, a low attrition rate virtually unheard of in BIA boarding schools.[51] A puzzling note was added to the report on dropouts: "Only one or two of these were deserters." Questions arise: Why the indefinite number? How did the "deserters" differ from other dropouts? The language used to refer to students in the Navajo Program is evidence of the persistence of the military structure, despite the goal of the Indian Reorganization Act to eliminate the military regimentation. In a report on the 1952–53 school year,, the military term "deserters" was echoed with the description "AWOL" (that is, absent without leave) appended to 5 dropouts from Sherman.[52]

From an enrollment of 738 that year, a total of 13 dropped out. In addition to the AWOL students, 1 left for military service, 3 returned home at their families' requests, 1 was sent home because of illness, 2 were sent to sanitariums for tuberculosis, and 1 went home simply on his own request. The dropout rate at Sherman was 2 percent, the lowest in the Navajo Program schools. There are, however, reports of students who went home at the close of a school year and did not return in the fall. These were identified as nonreturnees rather than dropouts. The rate of Sherman nonreturnees in 1952 was 17 percent, lower than five other schools and higher than three, and considered a relatively low rate of attrition.[53] The low percentage of students who permanently left the program was accounted for by the students being highly motivated by the vocational training, which was approved by their parents, and by the fact that the students "had received unremitting attention to their entire need."[54]

Despite the attention to their needs, some students had problems adjusting to boarding school life. Isabelle, a nineteen-year-old Navajo, was described as "self-conscious, very shy, speaks barely above a whisper, freezes when asked a question." Others, however, had positive experiences. During the same time, Corena, also a nineteen-year-old Navajo, was "well-behaved, dependable, participates, good leader, elected secretary of her class." On January 20, 1947, Hildegard Thompson, superintendent of Indian education of Navajos in the Chicago Office of Indian Affairs, recorded many positives: students behaved well, were respectful of property, worked well alone and with others, and had leadership qualities.[55]

Students who remained in the program and completed the basic courses in English language, math, and social skills were directed in their fourth year to the study of vocational work. Boys were assigned to courses in painting, carpentry, agriculture, baking, and institutional cooking. They were given overviews of possible vocations via scrapbooks with pictures of vocations, photographs, filmstrips, television, radio, newspapers, and magazines. Each vocation was covered in shops for five weeks, including field trips to working sites. Discussions about occupations stressed the importance of making the right decision. Factors to be considered included job and educational requirements; attitude toward employer, job, and coworkers; safety and health hazards; and wages, union fees, and insurance. Advantages and disadvantages of specific vocations were presented: location, city/country, indoors or out, day/night, split shifts, heights or low places, and the essential factor of job opportunities.[56]

There were ample training experiences in painting and carpentry on the Sherman campus. Evidently the unsightly condition of the campus facilities had appreciably affected teachers and staff to the degree that Runyan described the attitude of some as "defeatist."[57] By 1950, as part of their vocational education, students had made major improvements in the campus, including painting, reorganizing, and redecorating the dining room, auditorium, and classrooms. One job involved renovating a section of a dormitory, creating a "very nice apartment" for one of the dorm matrons. A highly successful extracurricular course, the Maintenance Hour, was shared by all pupils and all employees every weekday morning. Each employee at Sherman, together with eight or ten pupils, assumed care of a part of the campus. The success of the Maintenance Hour was evident in the improved morale of teachers and staff.[58]

Because Sherman had a new bakery, opportunities for on-the-job training in institutional baking and cooking were available on-campus as well as in the Riverside community. There was some concern about the "housekeeping details," with an admonition to maintain the highest standards of cleanliness. Opportunities for experience in agriculture were readily available on the Sherman Institute 110-acre farm, which provided food for the school as well as training for students. Despite the goal of preparing the students for urban employment, the Navajo Program was predicated on the expectation that the interest of the boys in agriculture would grow because there was considerable opportunity for it in the region of their reservation.[59]

A major attempt was made to merge classroom vocational instruction, summer job placement, and full-time placement in a continuous process. The first group of students at Sherman went home during the summer, but thereafter the objective was to place each student in a summer job. Efforts were made to place Sherman students in summer positions that might lead to permanent employment. In addition to jobs in cooking and baking, jobs were sought in woodwork, metalwork, automotive repair, leatherwork, and agriculture. The U.S. Forest Service also hired Sherman boys for fire suppression, trail clearing, and installing telephone lines.[60]

Students were placed in their fifth year at Sherman in intensive vocational training: the girls in home service, the boys in apprenticeships. The instruction for the girls included training in the use and care of electric equipment, such as vacuum cleaners, washers, dryers, and food mixers. A general service course prepared girls for work in hotels, restaurants, and "auto-courts."[61] Sherman also was the only school in the Navajo Program that had a course in Community School Housekeeping. A popular feature of this course was the planning and preparation of a dinner by one of the students, to which younger boys and girls with their teacher were invited. It was "party time" for the students who were "going out for dinner." The course was perceived as good training for the girls for the work of a "housekeeper on the reservation, although "going out for dinner" on a reservation would most likely be a communal experience, not relying on one host doing all the planning and preparation.[62]

The goals for home economics appear to have been bureaucratically demanding. A Sherman girl was required, among other accomplishments, to be able to make a variety of yeast breads, two kinds of cake (sponge and butter), two kinds of pie (cream and fruit), and two kinds of salad dressings (cooked and mayonnaise). They were also expected to be able to preserve fruits and vegetables by canning and drying, as well as to be proficient in proper laundry handling, house cleaning, child care, and the designing and sewing of a garment in wool.[63] It is doubtful whether most of these tasks would be useful on a reservation and questionable as to the type of urban employer who would require these achievements.

The goals for male vocational training also could be problematic. Despite the prior extensive instruction, some of the boys had cultural disadvantages not always understood by their employers. Those who had little or no prior experience working with the students were impatient with their limited English and skills. Assuming that the students knew fundamentals with which they had no familiarity, the employers were inclined to conclude the boys were "stupid."[64] Although the tasks were fundamental to employers, the vocabulary of the work could be difficult for the boys. Being apprenticed in metalwork, for example, meant that they were expected to know the uses of a scribe, how to solder copper, and the use of taps and dies. For general automotive work they were required to know the use of lug wrenches, dismounting irons, rubber mallets, cold chisels, box wrenches, and how to prepare plans for the procedure of an entire repair job.[65]

Sherman teachers and interpreters assumed the responsibility of helping students and employers adjust to each other, which became an essential component in successful job placement. The guiding principle was the conviction that the responsibility "did not end with the student getting a job and wishing him or her good luck. You stayed with them until the transition to the world of work was complete."[66] The success of the Navajo Program owed much to this resolute commitment by Sherman personnel.

Sherman superintendent Mythus Evans spent significant time using his natural diplomatic characteristics in making contacts and preparing the community for the employment of the students. He encouraged all members of the Sherman staff to make contacts and keep them interested in the students, ensuring that employment opportunities were cultivated. Sherman administration found that over time ingenuity and persistence with contacts did produce part-time employment and sometimes these jobs became permanent employment.[67]

In 1952–53, approximately one-third of the way through the fifteen-year program, sixty-eight Sherman graduates attained placement in the following jobs: twenty-five in home service, eight maids in hotels, six forestry workers, five busboys in resorts, four furniture factory workers, three kitchen/dining room workers, three farm/ranch workers, three house painters, three nursery workers (not specified as to plant or baby), three flight line mechanics, one hospital ward worker, one sash and door carpenter, one upholstery/drapery worker, and two craters in an aircraft company. In addition, two were in military service, two were in training as hospital ward attendants, and two were awaiting placement.[68] While most of these jobs were typical throughout the program, some graduates succeeded beyond expectations. One girl who began as a hospital ward attendant was promoted to a job in the operating room in charge of sterilizing equipment. Several boys who started as farmworkers showed aptitude with machinery and became operators of power equipment on roadwork.[69]

When students did become permanently employed, transitions in several areas of lifestyle were necessary. Sherman staff members were involved in helping students find appropriate housing, avoiding run-down neighborhoods they might select for reasons of economy or timidity. Representatives of the school introduced students to landlords, explaining their training and where they would be working. Accessibility of public transportations and churches, movies, parks, and YMCAs was a factor in selecting locations. If apartments were unfurnished, a

Sherman staff member would go with students to secondhand stores to find inexpensive furniture. Assistance was also provided with the matter of monthly bills for utilities and the demands of housekeeping and buying and preparing meals.[70]

Even housing with a family in the community presented difficulties. Two boys who had been placed with a lock company obtained housing and boarding with an elderly couple in an attractive home. After eating boarding school meals for five years, the boys felt awkward having meals at a small table with their hosts. They also had an uncomfortable learning experience with the bathtub, never having used one in the dormitory.[71] Aware of these potential difficulties, Sherman instructors had been stressing what they called the "fine points of living" as much as possible throughout the five-year course of study, but a handwritten note on a report by Runyan calls attention to the "need for proper facilities" for practice in the "fine points."[72]

In 1939, Sherman boys built seven cottages in an attempt by the administration to create a family atmosphere. A total of eleven boys and eleven girls of all ages lived in the seven cottages as a family, including the preparation of meals, under the supervision of a dorm matron or instructor. Alumni expressed positive attitudes about the program: it was "such a good experience" being self-sufficient in the cottages, learning how to get along with one another and accepting responsibility for their "family." They criticized the reason given for discontinuing the program that regular dormitory living gave the students more time to study, claiming that the cottage residents had "plenty of opportunity to study."[73]

Because of the "crash" nature of the Navajo Program, Sherman had not been able to completely prepare for the students. The budget was inadequate for hiring enough teacher-interpreters, and the teachers, interpreters, and staff personnel were not sufficiently prepared. There was a lack of appropriate educational material. The approach of the teachers was sometimes patriarchal and opinionated, as in the orientation course. Some of the goals, notably the expertise required of girls in home economics, were bureaucratically unreasonable.

Jon Ille in his study of the Navajo Program argues that it exemplified the federal Indian policy of termination and relocation. He adds, "While the Special Five Year Navajo Program at Sherman Institute provided industrial and service training for its participants, it failed to replace Navajo culture with Euro-American culture or create a large body of laborers in urban areas."[74] In contrast, in his evaluation of the Navajo Program, Superintendent Mythus Evans declared, "Truly a miracle has taken place."[75] This "miracle" must be recognized as being perceived from an assimilationist view.

It can be argued that the responses by Sherman Institute to the extraordinary demands of the Navajo Program were remarkably comprehensive. Considering the cultural, educational, and experiential differences of the Indian students, prolonged and acute homesickness could have been prevalent and the dropout rate excessive. The fact that both occurred relatively infrequently is a tribute to the fortitude and motivation of the students and the sensitivity of the teachers, interpreters, administrators, and staff of Sherman. Although the program did not create a large urban labor supply, a commendable accomplishment is manifest in the fact that the demand for employment of Sherman graduates exceeded the supply. The Navajo Program was more than twenty years ahead of the Bilingual Education Act of 1968, an offshoot of President Lyndon Johnson's War on Poverty, the first step toward recognition of students' Native languages and cultures.

The Navajo Program lasted for fifteen years, with a total of 4,330 students graduating and finding urban employment, one-fourth of them from Sherman.[76] Given the challenges of the goal to provide Indian youths who had no formal education sufficient vocational training and proficiency in English within five years to enable them to secure off-reservation jobs, the Sherman Navajo Program was as successful as it was innovative, ambitious, and bold.

♦♦♦♦

A unique group of students, the BIA Brats, lived on the Sherman Institute campus both before and during the time of the Navajo Project. The term "BIA Brats" was coined by Sherman administrators during the 1940s as an affectionate reference to the children of Bureau of Indian Affairs employees who worked at Sherman Institute. The BIA Brats, because of federal regulations, were not allowed to attend the Sherman school, but they lived on the campus throughout childhood. Of the thirty individuals constituting the BIA Brats, I interviewed nine, consisting of seven Indians and two Caucasians: Galen Townsend, Fort Bidwell Paiute and Owyhee Shoshone; Tonita Largo Glover and her daughter Lorene Sisquoc, both Fort Sill Apache and Mountain Cahuilla; Michele Meyers Conejo, Shoshone Bannock and Santa Rosa Cahuilla; Willetta Davis Goins and her grandson Jason Davis, both Hualapai and Pala Reservation; Melvin Campbell, Coyote Valley Pomo and Second Mesa Hopi; and Gary and Robert Evans, sons of Mythus Evans, the Caucasian superintendent of Sherman Institute from 1947 to 1969.

The BIA Brats vividly remember the Navajo students. Galen Townsend described the Navajo students' arrival:

> I would sit there with my friends and watch them arrive. It was a big deal. They had trucks here on campus that went up to the railroad [station] on Van Buren [Street] and brought [the students] back. There is a huge parking lot where they unloaded all the kids. They put the girls on one side and the boys on another. The classroom building was in the center, and on each side were two-story dormitories. Each student was assigned to a certain dorm, a certain floor, and a certain bed. The boys would come in cowboy hats and boots and Levi's. Some of the girls' blouses were brightly colored, and some were velvet. You could see the shininess. One thing I noticed was turquoise rings for the boys, and the girls had bracelets and necklaces. We listened to the supervisors, who were speaking Navajo, nothing but Navajo.[77]

The experience of growing up on the Sherman Institute campus has a special dimension for the Indian BIA Brats, demonstrating the middle course they chose between trying to integrate with the students and becoming assimilated in Riverside public schools. Lorene Sisquoc explained, "Sherman is our reservation. Most of us were relocated or our families were relocated here. Sherman is the place we could identify with, our back-home, our community."[78]

The BIA Brats especially contrast with the students enrolled in Sherman Institute before the Navajo Program began. The Brats and the students shared the campus. While the Brats embraced the concept

"Sherman is our reservation," many students, separated from their reservations, cultures, and families, perceived Sherman as a foreign environment and suffered acute homesickness.

The BIA Brats story is one of profound attachment to Sherman Institute. The bond persists through several generations—graduates becoming employees of Sherman, employees having children who became employees. Because so many of his relatives had attended Sherman Institute, Galen Townsend was keenly disappointed in not being able to attend the school. However, his family has maintained three generations of attachment to Sherman. His parents, Ross Townsend and Laura Premo Townsend, both graduated from Sherman Institute in 1930. Ross began working at the school immediately after graduation. Galen recalled, "Dad was hired as a carpenter's apprentice, but he also mastered plumbing, electrical work, paving, and roofing."[79]

Ross Townsend was also the wrestling coach, and in 1938 and 1939 he coached the best wrestling team in the history of Sherman Institute. From 1938 to 1944, Sherman had one of the best wrestling teams in the California Interscholastic Federation Southern California Section. Under Coach Townsend, Sherman students earned eleven individual championships in those years. Among the Indian wrestling champions were Milton Carro, Frank Burson, Willis Scribner, Leslie Ferris, Leonard Sanderson, Calvin Sisk, Reggie Townsend (Galen's uncle), Grover Moore, Leroy Alvarez, and Bernold Pollard.[80] In 1940–41, Ross Townsend also was assistant football coach.

Galen's mother began working as a matron in the dining hall in 1944 after the birth of Virgil, the youngest of her six BIA Brats. He remembered, "She was in the serving line showing the girls how to serve, and, of course, washing the trays. That was one thing Sherman really emphasized, cleanliness." Both of Galen's parents retired in 1960. Galen taught an arts and crafts class at Sherman from 1968 to 1972. His son Matthew is now the wrestling and baseball coach and his daughter Galene Townsend Miller is an instructor in computer science at Sherman.[81]

The family of Tonita Largo Glover and Lorene Sisquoc has a four-generation history with Sherman Institute. Their attachment began with Ida Gooday Largo, Fort Sill Apache, who worked as a dorm matron from 1951 to 1967. Her daughter Tonita Largo Glover lived on the campus during those years. If it had been allowed, her mother would have been intensely opposed to her daughter attending Sherman Institute, for Ida's education had been exclusively in boarding schools. "She had such negative experiences," Tonita said, "she vowed that she would never let her children attend boarding school." As with the other BIA Brats, Tonita went to Riverside public schools.[82] Tonita Glover began working at Sherman Institute in 1969 as a counselor's aide, later as a teacher's aide, substitute teacher, and education technician, and finally as a dorm supervisor for at-risk boys. Tonita's daughter Lorene lived on campus from 1969 to 1975. She started working at Sherman in 1982 and worked in the dorms from 1982 to 1995.[83]

Lorene began volunteering at Sherman Museum in 1985 helping Ramona K. Bradley, who established the museum. Sisquoc recalled, "I spent four years with her. It's where I got my training." Lorene has great respect for Bradley, a Caucasian, who was, in Sisquoc's words, "Indian in her heart." Ramona Bradley died in 1989, and the museum was closed for two years. In 1991, Lorene was asked to be the volunteer curator. While she was working in the dorm and volunteering in the museum, she also was teaching a basketry class in the Freshman Focus program. Meanwhile, she initiated an outreach program for local reservations and communities. Finally, Sherman created a position comprising the responsibilities in which Lorene was already involved, and she became the curator of the Sherman Indian Museum and the Cultural Tradition Leader of the school in 2000.[84] Tonita Glover said, "It's the tradition, carried over from my mother to me, to Lorene and now to my granddaughter Tonita Marie Maciel. She is secretary to the vice-principal, Carl Davis. There are four generations that have worked here at Sherman."[85]

Michele Meyers Conejo's parents both graduated from Sherman Institute in 1939. Her mother, Emily Matsaw Meyers, a Shoshone Bannock, had enrolled at Sherman at age fourteen, when her sister Effie had been there three years. Their uncle Ray Pocatello also attended Sherman. Michele's father, William Meyers, and his brother John, both Santa Rosa Cahuilla, had enrolled as very young children. Emily and William were married in 1945, and Michele was born in 1946. Emily Meyers worked at Sherman Institute from 1952 until 1960 as a matron in the boys' dorm Alexander and also taught an arts and crafts class.[86]

Willetta Davis Goins's mother, Naomi Brittain, a Hualapai, worked as a dorm matron, and her stepfather, Maurice Brittain, from the Pala Reservation, worked in the boiler room from 1942 to 1952. The attachment Naomi and Maurice Brittain had for Sherman was continued through their grandson, Jason Davis, who worked as a counselor from 2002 to 2009.[87]

A unique attachment to Sherman is apparent in the perspectives of BIA Brat brothers Gary and Robert Evans. In addition to their father serving as superintendent of Sherman Institute, their mother, Mae Evans, was postmaster in the post office, located in the building that is now the museum. Gary was five years old and Robert was three when they began living on the campus, and both have strong positive memories of growing up on the campus, socializing with the students and with the other BIA Brats.[88]

The BIA Brats lived an idyllic life on the Sherman campus. Michele Conejo said, "I considered Sherman home, that's for sure."[89] Willetta Goins described Sherman as a huge playground: "A wonderful, wonderful playground!"[90] However, on the same campus, during the years before the Navajo Program, the students were vulnerable, being separated from their home, language, and family, subjected to strict discipline, and required to learn a behavior appropriate to an unfamiliar environment. While students in the Navajo Program had a very low rate of dropouts, other students in the earlier years had many reasons for dropping out. Typical dropouts were students ranging in age from fourteen to eighteen who returned to their reservations because they were needed at home. The most frequently documented reason for students' dropping out was "plain homesickness."[91] Sherman superintendents addressed the issue by sending letters to parents of the students, stating, "Frequently new students become homesick after their arrival and write their parents asking them to send money for the fare home. If you would write encouraging your student to remain for a month or six weeks before leaving instead of sending money for a ticket, you would help your child become adjusted. In most cases before a month has passed, the child has become adjusted and contented."[92]

Despite the superintendents' optimistic prediction, longing for home reservations was a persistent and serious issue. Dorm supervisors Emily Meyers, Tonita Largo Glover, Naomi Brittain, Jason Davis, and Walter and Margaret Campbell all reported distressing homesickness among the students.[93] Willetta Goins pointed out another major difference in the lives of the students: "We [BIA Brats] didn't have certain times to be in, certain times to go to dinner, certain times to do this or that, like the dorm kids did."[94] Viola Martinez, who attended Sherman Institute from 1927 to 1932, described the daily routine of the school:[95]

> At 6:00 A.M. there was this triangle thing. It was a good-sized triangle and you could hear it throughout the dorms. The triangle got us up, then in forty-five minutes, it would go again. This meant "Out front. Line up." From there you would go to the dining room, which was quite a way from the dorm.... Breakfast at 7:00. You were given forty-five minutes to eat your breakfast. Line up again and go back to the dormitories. Get ready for school. At 9:00 you were ready to go to your first class. Those that were going to work would go to their work projects. Line up. Go to the group you were involved with. Then at 11:30 a regular siren would go off to let everybody know that it would be time to eat in a half hour. You would go back to your dorms and line up. At 12:00 line up, then go back to the dining room for lunch. Then at 12:30, line up and go back to the dorms. At 1:00 you went to your afternoon detail. Those that were in school in the morning would go to work, and those that were working in the morning would go to the classrooms. Dismissal was usually around 4:00. You would line up and go back to your respective dorms. You had about an hour and a half free time before lining up for dinner. Of course after dinner you had your study hours.... At 9:00 you had to be ready for bed.

This regimentation was a strong factor in causing a degree of separation between the children of employees and the students. Galen Townsend remembered, "We weren't allowed to mingle with the students, but we played a lot of basketball against them and this is how we met them." Tonita Largo Glover similarly recalled living and playing on campus but being kept separate from the students: "We were told we couldn't be around them so we didn't." Mel Campbell, though, was able to circumvent the imposed separation, possibly because his father and mother, Walter and Margaret, were dorm supervisors. Mel remembered doing what a "normal teenager" would do, including visiting friends in the dorms in the evening: "There was no tight security and everyone knew us."[96]

Michele Conejo recalled having attended dances at Sherman. However, a meeting of department heads during this time indicated dissatisfaction with the children of employees attending the dances. Separation of BIA Brats and students was also evident in another conclusion of the department heads regarding employees' teenage girls: "The Gym may be used by BRATS only when the students are not. Also the BRATS should not use the students' living rooms for a place to gather."[97]

There was a prohibition against BIA Brats dating Sherman students. "Even though we were all Indian," Michele said, "dating wasn't part of the students' education."[98] Lorene recalled, "I had crushes on tons of boys, but I don't think they ever knew I did. I was a fourteen-year-old kid."[99] In stark contrast to Lorene, students Julia (age seventeen), Mari Louise (age sixteen), and Pauline and Lila (both age fourteen) dropped out of Sherman because they were pregnant.[100] Whether they became pregnant before or after they entered Sherman, the disparity in regard to sexual experience is valid. The BIA Brats were sheltered; the students were vulnerable.

The descriptions by the BIA Brats of their conflicts with parents and administrators are tame. For Galen and his friends, having the run of the campus during the summer when the students were gone meant getting into buildings to find out what the students did in them. "The windows were open," he said. "We'd just slide through and look around." In a dormitory, there were mattresses on the floor, and he and his friends were caught diving on them. "They assigned us work duty on the campus." For about a month Galen and friends helped a groundskeeper pick up trash. "That's all we did." About having the run of the campus in the summer, Robert Evans laughed and said, "Yes, absolutely. Maybe more run than we should have had." He particularly recalled "mischief" with BB guns—not with students but with other BIA Brats.[101]

Lorene Sisquoc said, "We did things that if we had been caught we would have been in trouble. We'd spray hairspray and light a match to it."

As she became a little older, however, she was, in her own description, a naughty girl: "I was always getting in trouble, and I got sent to an Indian Camp in Topanga Canyon. It was set up to continue the old ways and resist the mainstream bad stuff." While there, she asked to be given an Indian name, and Grandfather Semu gave her the name Sisquoc, a Chumash word for quail. She told me, "I have associated with the quail since I was fifteen."[102] Lorene's misbehavior does not quite compare with that of troubled students, and the remedy for her delinquency was constructive.

The misconduct of the students attending classes at Sherman Institute was often more severe, as in the case of Lloyd, a fifteen-year-old, who was being held by the juvenile authorities of Riverside because he was implicated in a car theft. His remaining at Sherman was in jeopardy. Documents in the National Archive illustrate that problems with alcohol and drugs were a major challenge in the dorms. A letter in the files of Sherman Institute from Leonard Frazier, dormitory supervisor, states, "Norman ... came back from Los Angeles last night about 12:00 P.M. He was very drunk and he slept all Sunday morning.... Norman said he got his drinks from some Army boys in Los Angeles. He also brought back about three-hundred pennies, he said he got them from his uncle."[103] The pennies may be partly explained by a report written by staff member Ethelyn Miller: "Norman was always neat and clean, taking great pride in his personal appearance.... He would seem very despondent when he did not have money to spend."[104]

Another report reveals an unexplained change in the behavior of sixteen-year-old Esther. Two months after her arrival at Sherman she was described as "[w]ell-behaved, a leader under supervision, persistent, hard, accurate worker, wholesome & constructive, dependable, neat, clean, trustworthy with property and in word." Four months later the description changed: "Esther needs constant supervision, slow and careless, not responsible, personally dishonest, deceitful, careless in person and dress, indifferent, passive, doesn't work well with others."[105] Perhaps, like Norman, Esther became depressed over the lack of spending money; possibly homesickness caught up with her or there were distressing problems on her reservation.

When Jason Davis, the son of BIA Brat Willetta Goins, worked as a counselor at Sherman, he found that Sherman was also a safe haven for some students, for whom "a lot of healing need[ed] to occur." There is a similarity between these students and the BIA Brats. The concept of being safe is repeated in the interviews with the Brats. Michele Meyers Conejo, for example, recalled, "I always had the feeling of security when I was a child. Our boundaries were all four corners of the campus. Only the employees could come onto the campus." Willetta regretted that her children growing up in Los Angeles did not have the sheltered environment she had. Galen related the perception of being safe: "This is our home. No one can come in and bother us."[106]

Applications for admission to Sherman Institute filed by social services agencies reveal at-risk children who would find a sanctuary at Sherman. In 1945, many fathers who were veterans returning from military action in World War II could not find work and maintain a home for their children. A report about ten-year-old Elma May, who was identified as "½ Mission Indian," states, "This child had been made a ward of the San Bernardino County Court because of unfit parents, drunkards, beyond reform. Father refuses to work, child is undernourished." Her sister Roberta (also ten) was described as half starved; one brother, Angel Buddie (age fifteen), was "underfed and not properly dressed"; and another brother, Gilbert (age sixteen), was also "underfed and wearing what are basically rags."[107] Julia Hyde (twelve years old) resided opposite an army camp. A report concerning her states, "Soldiers come to the house all night long for purposes that are anything but pure. Her father is dead, her stepfather is serving time for killing Julia's brother." The conclusion of the report about Elma May would apply to all of these at-risk children: "Sherman Institute will be a real home to this unfortunate waif."[108]

The response to these acute problems and those of lesser severity by the dorm supervisors, who were parents of BIA Brats, must have let some light into the lives of the troubled students. Although such incidents were rare, some students were so disturbed that Mel Campbell remembered his parents had to call the police. Mel said of his mother, "Despite the difficulties, she loved Sherman. She loved the kids. She gave a lot, but she received a lot." Margaret Campbell stayed for over twenty years, from 1940 through the 1960s, also volunteering as an assistant to the curator of Sherman Museum. Michele Conejo remembered that her mother liked her work as a supervisor in the boys' dorm so much, despite the problems, that she convinced a couple of friends to work at Sherman. Willetta Goins remembered that her mother also "loved the kids" and "if she had her way would have worked forever." Tonita Glover recalled working with students at-risk for alcohol abuse: "We did counseling, we gave them extra duty hours in the dorm, we monitored to keep them sober, we had programs like AA." When none of these efforts were successful, Tonita used a different approach that was effective: "I ran my dorm in a traditional Native way, to let our students know of their traditions." Despite the demanding responsibility of at-risk students, Tonita proclaimed that Sherman was where she wanted to be. "Sherman Institute was my environment. I always wanted to stay with my own people. I was happy with my job here."[109]

The first job of Tonita's daughter Lorene Sisquoc was as a matron in Woodlawn Dorm. "That's the older boys' dorm," she said. "I was twenty-two and they were eighteen, nineteen, twenty-year-olds, and I was telling them to clean their rooms, make their beds, that kind of stuff. For me it was the best thing in my life. It changed my life. I remember being really close to them like a sister. I am real happy for that part of my life. I was never cussed out, except when somebody was intoxicated. They would come back the next day and apologize. I still am meeting some of them now on Facebook. They have posted 'You were such a Mom, the one that listened to us.'"[110]

♦♦♦♦

Despite a schedule devoted to studies and work, and despite severe homesickness, students had an impressive variety of extracurricular activities: picnics, trips to Knott's Berry Farm, attending plays at Riverside Junior College, and dances at the gym, for which "the boys called for the young ladies and brought them home." Teachers and counselors planned learning activities, such as amateur hours "to help the students realize what English can be gained from an activity of that type." The girls planned and prepared teas for members of the community, described as "wonderful experiences for the girls," who "showed improvement [in social skills] with each tea party."[111]

Despite the separation of BIA Brats and students, there must have been ways to share experiences even off-campus. When asked if he had made friends with Sherman students, Mel Campbell responded, "Oh yeah! My best friends are former students. Now that I'm older I appreciate them even more." Michele Conejo remembered going to movies with students in nearby Arlington. She stressed, "The people I know from Sherman are good people. As I grew older, the friendships became more important to me." Gary Evans recalled having students as friends, meeting them when they played basketball and football together. He also belonged to a Boy Scout troop sponsored by Sherman for both the students and the children of employees. His brother Robert also spoke of bonding with students through sports activities. In concurrence with other BIA Brats, he said, "I couldn't have had a better place to grow up, a marvelous, marvelous experience, very valuable, and a natural thing."[112]

The continuation of attachment to Sherman by BIA Brats becoming employees is dramatically evident in four generations of the family of Lorene Sisquoc. The connection to Sherman, begun by Ida Gooday Largo in 1951 and continued by Tonita Largo Glover beginning in 1969, is presently demonstrated by Lorene Sisquoc and her daughter Tonita Marie Maciel. Lorene perceives it as "a path set out before [her]." She is deeply committed to teaching at Sherman and to her community outreach, creating Mother Earth (a community youth group) and an elders program at Sherman. In the year 2000, at the urging of Donna Largo (a Cahuilla basket maker who is Lorene's distant cousin), she founded Nexwetem, the Southern California Basket Weavers. Tonita Marie began working at Sherman in 2004 as a home living assistant in Wauneka Dormitory for freshman girls and has been academic secretary since 2005.[113]

Galen Townsend expresses considerable pride in his family's lasting involvement with Sherman. The attachment, begun with his parents Ross and Laura Premo Townsend, who graduated from Sherman in 1930, then worked there until 1967, is currently continued by Galen's son Matthew and daughter Galene. The second generation of connection was demonstrated by Galen when he returned to Riverside from military service in Germany and applied for a position at Sherman.

His special extracurriculum program in arts and crafts from 1968 to 1972 "was something [he] was doing for the kids." He said, "I really enjoyed it." In addition to his parents, Galen's aunts Juanita and Beatrice Townsend and his uncles Warner and Willis Premo attended Sherman Institute. Galen himself has been a volunteer in the Sherman Museum since 2008. Willetta Goins said that her association with students and other BIA Brats made her "feel special being Native." She has evidently passed this feeling on to her son Jason, who wants his son to attend Sherman "just for the Indian experience."[114]

It can be argued that because of their idyllic life and the generational continuity, the attachment to Sherman expressed by the BIA Brats is to be expected. In addition to affection, however, they also express significant insights gained from their experiences at Sherman. Mel Campbell, for example, stated, "Over the years they've said they're going to close Sherman. I hope that never happens. Indian kids need schools like this. There's a lot of history at Sherman. Traditions are being carried on. That's the way it should be."[115]

Michele Conejo, likewise, said, "The best experiences I have had have been meeting a lot of different Indians that have made me aware of cultural differences. Indians have pride in their culture." Jason Davis had considerable praise for Sherman: "I grew up an urban Indian, and though we visited our reservation a lot, my real exposure was when I worked at Sherman for seven years. It really gave me a better sense of identity, responsibility, and understanding of the present and past struggles."[116]

Tonita Glover said, "Our young people need places like Sherman to have an education. I used to tell that to my students: 'Get an education. Go all the way to get your education whether it be vocational or higher education. You have to live in the white man's world. It's not like it was way back when. It's getting more high tech than ever.'"[117]

Lorene Sisquoc referred to a multilayered attachment: "At boarding school people form tribal networks through marriages, through friendships. Even students who had bad experiences have some positive feelings because of the friendships they made or because someone at Sherman made a difference in their lives."[118]

Gary Evans believes that he has become more sympathetic to the problems Indians have faced: "I am proud of the [Indian] friends I have made." Robert Evans believes he gained an appreciation for "people of color," and he is very proud to have had that privilege. His experiences at Sherman gave him "a love and appreciation, a binding and bonding that was very, very valuable and still is."[119]

This enhanced appreciation of diverse Indian cultures is expressed by all of the interviewees, a testament to the power of their socializing, although not integrating, with Indians on the Sherman campus. The interviews of this small, undocumented group of the BIA Brats reveal a profound paradox in the history of Sherman Institute. During the years following World War II, there was a significant renewal of pressure to assimilate Indians. Students, including those in the Navajo Program, were once again physically and intellectually removed from their cultures, while BIA Brats were being drawn deeper into their Indian identity to the remarkable extent that they consider Sherman their reservation.

The Navajo Special Education Program presents another paradox. While the Navajos were being educated bilingually, there was growing conservative demand to return to the "old" boarding school programs of English-only instruction, an attitude that had some support by Indians. Navajo tribal leader Chee Dodge sent a letter to the House Select Committee to Investigate Indian Affairs and Conditions urging that the Navajo language no longer be taught in government schools because Navajos needed to learn English to compete in employment. Similarly, Navajo Tribal Councilman Hoskie Cronemeyer argued for a return to the "very good" boarding schools where English-only was mandated. He also requested abolishing the teaching of Navajo customs, which "we already know."[120]

In 1952, Hildegard Thompson succeeded Willard Beatty as BIA director of education, a position she held for thirteen years, during the administrations of three commissioners: Dillon Myer, Glenn Emmons, and Philleo Nash.[121] She served as director during one of the most demanding periods of Indian education, years during which the Office of Indian Education struggled with the results of hasty and ill-planned congressional legislation.

3

Termination—"Tragedy" and "Challenge"

1953–1972

The renewed emphasis on assimilation during the administrations of Harry Truman and Dwight Eisenhower, when Dillon S. Myer was commissioner of Indian Affairs, resulted in a historic Indian affairs policy, which caused significant and long-lasting damage. In 1953 Congress adopted House Concurrent Resolution 108, which established the policy of terminating the relationship between the federal government and Indian people, ending the government's responsibility for social, economic, and educational services. Congress argued that poverty conditions on the reservations were caused by BIA mismanagement and that some tribes would be better off with independence.[1]

The appointment by Eisenhower of Glenn L. Emmons to succeed Myer as commissioner continued the policy of termination. Between 1953 and 1964, 109 tribes were terminated, and only 4 regained federal recognition.[2] An adjunct policy, intended to bring Indians into postwar prosperity, relocated Indians for employment opportunities from rural to urban locations, including Chicago, Seattle, Minneapolis, and Los Angeles. Many Indians who relocated were not trained for available jobs or prepared for urban life. While some Indians returned to their reservations and others made successful transitions to cities, urban ghettos were an unfortunate result of this assimilationist effort.[3] The relocation policy was referred to by Lorene Sisquoc in explaining why the BIA Brats considered Sherman their reservation.

Termination and relocation had a major impact on Indian education. Congruent with the government's policy of removing Indians from reservations into urban industrial work, Hildegard Thompson's policy was to move Indian children from boarding schools into public schools to prepare them for an urban technological society. An academic-oriented curriculum in high school and post–high school vocational training provided Indian students with two options: college or occupational training.[4] Following the completion of the Navajo Program, Sherman Institute resumed a standard high school curriculum in 1962 and became an accredited high school in 1971.[5]

Thompson was subjected to pressure from Indian people to restore the old vocational programs and insistence from academicians to make high school a college preparatory course. During her tenure, there was a significant increase in the number of Indian students enrolled in post–high school education, either college or vocational training. However, Indians' widespread opposition or indifference to Thompson's programs was a censure of the hasty and ill-planned termination and relocation policy.[6]

During the 1960s, life had changed somewhat for the better at Sherman Institute. Philleo Nash visited the campus in November 1961 and complimented the students on their accomplishments.[7] Students had good summer jobs, including work at national parks and in commercial baking. Student income from Saturday outing jobs had increased, although no information is given as to how many students were involved.[8] During the month of September 1962, boys earned $2,417 and girls earned $2,004.[9] From the Save the Children Federation, boys received $961 and girls $558.[10] The $1,461 sent from home for girls was notably more than the $961 sent for boys.[11] Combined, boys and girls spent $2,289 for clothing, the girls spending $378 more than the boys.[12]

When asked in 1962 what they thought about Sherman, students were quite positive. "It's a nice, warm and clean place, green and pretty. I have many friends. I like the teachers too. They teach me many things and they help me to be good." One student said she was told by a friend that Sherman was the "number one" school and added, "I'm joyful. What my friend said is all true."[13]

Unlike Truman and Eisenhower, President John F. Kennedy (1961–63) recommended ending the termination policy. The appointment of Philleo Nash as commissioner in 1961 marked the beginning of the decline of termination. When Hildegard Thompson retired in 1965, the pendulum was swinging back to anti-assimilation, toward Indian self-determination.[14] On April 11, 1965, Congress passed the Elementary and Secondary Education Act (ESEA), which provided funds for BIA schools under Title I of the act.[15] Title I was designed to provide funding for educating educationally disadvantaged students. Congress budgeted more than 80 percent of the funds originally appropriated under the ESEA for Title I programs. The bureau submitted proposals for projects to the U.S. Office of Education for approval.[16] Sherman received funds for ten projects: (1) recreation programs for nights and weekends; (2) apartment living with work education; (3) night and weekend arts and crafts instruction; (4) field trips; (5) a reading lab; (6) parent visitation; (7) a second reading lab; (8) specialized progressive physical and life sciences; (9) adapted physical education and fitness; and (10) Junior Marine ROTC.[17]

Commissioner Nash, who represented the departure from the termination policy, was respected by the National Congress of American Indians, but Secretary of the Interior Stewart Udall became frustrated with Nash for not stimulating Indian industrial development. Their conflict hastened Nash's resignation in 1966.[18] In April 1966, President Lyndon Johnson, determined to "erase old attitudes of paternalism and promote Indian self-help," appointed as commissioner of Indian Affairs Robert L. Bennett, an Oneida and a Haskell graduate, the first Indian to hold that office since Ely Parker (1869–71), a Seneca.[19] Bennett had supported relocation in 1964, when he was BIA area director for Alaska. In an article written with L. Madison Coombs, education specialist for the BIA, Bennett claimed that it was inevitable for young Indians to leave their reservations for metropolitan areas and that it was "the job of the Bureau of Indian Affairs to prepare them to do this."[20] As commissioner, though, he argued actively for a policy that deemphasized relocation, declaring, "[S]elf-determination should be the fire to rekindle in the hearts of the first Americans."[21]

Udall's frustration with the Bureau of Indian Affairs during Nash's administration had been intensified by political pressure from both houses of Congress to support Indian control of development and self-determination in education.[22] Concern for Sherman Institute was manifested by Congressman John V. Tunney of California in 1967 and Senators Paul Fannin of Arizona and Robert Kennedy of New York in 1968.[23]

In particular, Tunney sought federal assistance to alleviate a critical building need: eight structures on the Sherman campus had been closed because they did not meet the earthquake safety standards of the State of California. Tunney said he would confer with Commissioner Bennett as to why Sherman's building projects had been lowered on the priority list.[24] A campaign initiated by Gordon Addison, publisher of the *Arlington Times,* and the Arlington Chamber of Commerce had requested Tunney's support. Addison pointed out that Sherman's annual budget of $1,400,000 benefited the Riverside economy.[25] Moreover, he argued, "Saturday employment for the Sherman boys and girls, not only gives valuable job training, but generates an estimated $50,000 income for the youths, most of which is spent here. Over $30,000 in student moneys is on deposit in local savings accounts. Children also receive money from family and tribal assets, and the Save the Children Federation sends over $11,000 annually to some 150 underprivileged Indians to assist in their material and clothing."[26]

The campaign resulted in a visit to Sherman Institute by Will Rogers, Jr., assistant to Commissioner Robert Bennett. Rogers spoke to an outdoor assembly of students and staff, stating, "It is our hope that this will be the last group of students to have assemblies in open air. We hope that we can get you a proper building for recreation, for basketball games, for assemblies. We are trying to get the money out of Washington." Rogers told the audience that his grandfather had been a leader of the Cherokee tribe in Oklahoma and his father, the celebrated Will Rogers, Sr., had gone to "an Indian school in Oklahoma" and represented a "success story for all Indians." He then spoke directly to the students about the "changing Indian picture," declaring that he did not like "the typical shyness and humility in Indian boys and girls." He told them, "I want you to develop pride in yourselves."[27]

A few days later, on November 1, 1967, Congressman Tunney told the *Arlington Times* that he was assured by Commissioner Bennett of the Department of Indian Affairs that he would submit to the Budget and Appropriations Committee a request for $40,000 to build a multipurpose prefabricated building for the Sherman campus. However, because of the "tight federal fiscal condition," Bennett made no promise as to when the crucial campus building program would be completed. Meanwhile, he would attempt to lease a tent large enough for assemblies on the Sherman campus.[28]

Senators Robert Kennedy and Paul Fannin visited Sherman Institute on January 5, 1968, as key members of the Senate Special Subcommittee on Indian Education, newly created in response to congressional pressure for Indian self-determination. After introductory remarks by Superintendent Mythus Evans, student body president Webster Hogan (a Mohave from Parker, Arizona) welcomed the senators to Sherman. After a presentation by the Sherman chorus, singing "Blowing in the Wind" and "Soon Ah Will Be Done," student body vice president Sam Nephew (a Navajo of Kayenta, Arizona) introduced Senator Fannin. Senator Kennedy was introduced by Cecelia Charley (a Navajo from Shiprock, New Mexico).[29]

In the Sherman Indian Museum Archive are photocopies of Cecelia's remarks and of her copy of the program for the senators' visit, which is covered with autographs and compliments, including that of Superintendent Evans: "You have made a real contribution to Sherman. We all appreciate your efforts. Good Luck."

Cecelia's introductory comments follow:

> My name is Cecelia Charley. I come from the Navajo Reservation and Shiprock, New Mexico. We couldn't find any New York Indians here, so I'm going to introduce Senator Kennedy. Robert Kennedy is a name known to all of us. He is the brother of our late president. He is a former Attorney General of the United States. He has held many political offices. He was born in Boston, and he has always lived his life in big cities. But he has traveled over many of our reservations. A few days ago he was in Ft. Hall, Idaho, holding hearings on Indian schools in that state. Now he is here in Riverside to look at the needs of our school. Mr. Kennedy we do need our gymnasium! It is a pleasure for a Navajo from New Mexico to introduce an Irishman from New York!!! The Honorable Robert F. Kennedy, from the State of New York!

The photocopy of her speech is signed by Robert Kennedy with an acknowledgment that is no longer entirely legible but is most likely "With appreciation."

Gordon Addison described the visit in the *Arlington Times* as a "tumultuous senatorial stopover." Supervisor Evans told the *Times* that although he was sure much good would come from the visit, he regretted that the limited time of the visit "did not allow school officials to sit down quietly with the senators to explain all the problems and needs of Sherman." Both senators investigated the curriculum, teaching materials, and campus facilities with the goal of assessing the facts about the operation of the school. Kennedy expressed concern over the lack of books on Indian history and traditions in the small library. Superintendent Evans responded that the annual $6,000 budget for books funded only the texts offered in the local public schools. The senators conveyed the most approval for the work of students being trained in mechanical drawing; in particular, they commended instructor Al Rhodes on students' house plans and other drafting exhibits that had won awards at the Indio Date Festival.[30]

While they observed classes in carpentry, metal shop, typing, and homemaking, they repeatedly stated to faculty and students that they saw a need for students to be educated in professional fields, especially teaching. Superintendent Evans told the *Times* that the academic progress of Sherman students had been "amazing." In 1966, for example, 28 percent of the graduates had gone on to university, junior college, or advanced vocational training. In 1967, 64 percent of the graduates enrolled in post–high school education. At an assembly, again outdoor, Senator Fannin, former governor of Arizona, told the audience that 27 percent of the land in his home state was owned by Indians and that he was particularly anxious to give students better opportunities to help themselves. He expressed his fondest hope: "Indians will be motivated to take their place in the community as doctors, lawyers, and above all, teachers." He also commended the students on their good attitude in spite of building shortages, inadequate budgets, and overcrowded conditions on the campus.

Senator Kennedy began somewhat awkwardly by saying, "You are the first citizens, the ones who made the United States." He continued more appropriately: "The Indians were promised an adequate education, but those treaties have been broken. It requires a commitment of the executive and legislative branches, the country as a whole, and above all, a commitment to your community, your tribe, your state and your country." After giving an emphatic clap of his hands, he promised, "We pledge ourselves to make efforts for improvement at this Institute and in Indian schools across the country."[31]

On January 30, 1968, the *Sherman Bulletin* reported that Tunney had informed Superintendent Evans that Commissioner Bennett had received authorization from the Budget and Appropriations Committee for the requested funds and bids were being solicited for the construction of a prefab gym/auditorium. Tunney commended members of the community for bringing Sherman Institute's needs to the forefront, stating, "This should be the beginning of the community's efforts to see that proper facilities are available at the Institute."[32] There is no documentation that the visit to Sherman Institute by Senators Kennedy and Fannin had an effect on the budget approval for the building; however, Senator Kennedy's promise made at the assembly became reality when the Special Subcommittee on Indian Education, with his leadership, initiated a comprehensive investigation of Indian education throughout the nation.

The genesis of this special subcommittee may be traced to the Education Subcommittee on Labor and Public Welfare. Senator Fannin in a letter to Senator Wayne Morse of Oregon, chairman of the Education Subcommittee on Education, urged the establishment of a Special Subcommittee on Indian Education. With the enthusiastic endorsement of Senator Morse and Senator Lister Hill of Alabama, the special subcommittee was established with Senator Robert Kennedy of New York serving as chairman from August 25, 1967 to June 6, 1968.[33]

The rationale for the investigation was movingly articulated by Senator Kennedy:

> To a substantial extent, the quality and effectiveness of Indian education is a test of this Government's understanding and commitment. The few statistics we have are the most eloquent evidence of our own failure: Approximately 16,000 children are not in school at all; dropout rates are twice the national average. . . . Indian children, more than any other group, believe themselves

to be "below average" in intelligence. . . . Indian children in the 12th grade have the poorest self-concept of all minority groups tested. Indian income is $1500—75% below the national average; his unemployment rate is ten times the national average.

These facts are cold statistics which illuminate a national tragedy and a national disgrace. They demonstrate that the "First American" had become the last American with the opportunity for employment, education, a decent income, and the chance for a fulfilling and rewarding life.

This subcommittee does not expect to unveil any quick and easy answers to this dilemma. But, clearly, effective education lies at the heart of any lasting solution. And it must be an education that no longer presumes that cultural differences mean cultural inferiority.[34]

The investigation was launched with five fundamental principles:

1. The failure of Indian education has deep historical roots and is closely interrelated with a general failure of national policy.
2. The failure of Indian education must be examined in the context of the most severe poverty confronting any minority group in the United States.
3. Indian education is a cross-cultural transaction. The failure must be examined in terms of its complexity of causes and psychological and social effects.
4. Indian education has evolved into a controversial and unique institution, the Federal Boarding School which deserves special attention and concern.
5. Indian education takes place in a great diversity of geographical and cultural settings.[35]

In response to all five items, but particularly the special attention needed to investigate Indian boarding schools, the subcommittee authorized the investigation of the fourteen schools, including Sherman Institute. Senator Morse served as chairman from June 14, 1968, to January 3, 1969, following Robert Kennedy's assassination, and Edward Kennedy completed his brother's work on the special subcommittee, serving as chair from February 1, 1969, until the final report was issued November 3, 1969.[36] The summary report of the subcommittee, filling seven volumes, was entitled *Indian Education: A National Tragedy, a National Challenge*.[37]

"[A] rigid, uncompromising, bureaucratic, authoritarian, non-innovative, feudal barony." This caustic depiction of Sherman Institute has been extensively quoted in the scholarship on Indian boarding schools. It was written by Elwin Svenson, then vice-chancellor at UCLA, who was authorized to investigate Sherman Institute by the Senate Special Subcommittee on Indian Education. He visited the school for two days in 1968, then wrote a thirteen-page criticism. The seven-volume summary report of the subcommittee was substantially based on the evaluation of Svenson and those of investigators of thirteen other federal Indian boarding schools.

In submitting the report to Senator Morse, Svenson advised him to consider the report as "draft statements," since he had not reread the report since its initial preparation. Further, Svenson stated, "Let me say that one should be wary of the 2-day visit to a 66-year-old institution which results in a recriminatory and scurrilous report. Such a visit necessarily omits the composite experiences of the school, the history of successes and failures, and problems of community relations and the changing of staff and population." He compared the investigation with a "snapshot" in which "distortions can well be raised."[38] More than forty years later, when asked whether a longer visit would have proved more favorable, he responded, "It would have provided more data but no change."[39]

His dissatisfaction with the conditions at Sherman was repeatedly expressed, particularly when he summarized the inadequacies in the cover letter (159–60):

1. Inadequate outside evaluation of the school
2. Inadequate staff, both quantitative and qualitative [He describes the staff as "giving the impression of creaky old age."]
3. Inadequate administrative skill in budgeting, use of surplus property
4. Inadequate vigor in defending the interests of students

5. Inadequate admissions criteria
6. Inadequate feed-back of results
7. Inadequate funding
8. Inadequately identified goals
9. Inadequate vocational training
10. Inadequate buildings

"Other than that most everything is OK" (160).

Svenson identified in more detail disturbing conditions at Sherman Institute in need of significant attention by the federal government. In response to the question of whether Sherman's program relates to the fact that the students are reservation Indians, the report cites a "disquieting factor" that a substantial number of the students were assigned to Sherman for "sociological reasons which have little or nothing to do with education. . . . Broken homes, orphans, antisocial behavior, alcoholism of parents, etc." (160).

Svenson's frustration with Sherman is evident in statement after statement. The "appalling" lack of textbooks was exceeded by the "helpless approach" of the staff. The 75 cents per day per student for food produced a "monotonous" diet that was "inappropriate for this age population" (158–59). The lack of communication skills—speaking, listening, reading, and writing—was the greatest problem, while there was no "tutorial effort" or "staff attention" devoted to it (161). The dormitory counseling program did not meet the minimum safety requirements of the BIA, which Svenson considered "a potentially dangerous situation" (164). The shops and labs were using "limited" machines and tools of World War II vintage (165). Eight buildings had been condemned as unsafe according to California earthquake standards, resulting in "inefficient and awkward" space usage. The library was one of the condemned buildings, but as one staff member seriously commented, since hardly anyone uses it, the building is being continued in use to store books (165).

Pertinent to the Special Subcommittee's concern with "the general failure of the national policy," Svenson referred to the funds allocated to Sherman being "apparently a function of availability rather than the result of intelligent budgeting and planning"(159). Further, the staffing design authorized by the government was "inadequate by any measurement."

In relation to the education of Indian students being a cross-cultural transaction, Svenson found deficiencies in two critical areas: the teachers at Sherman, while fulfilling the requirements of the State of California, "lack[ed] the ability to cope with the special student population"; and there was no language program at Sherman for students with limited English skills (162, 164).

Moreover, Svenson commented negatively on aspects of Sherman's program that at first appear to be positive. He observed that the formal requirements for teachers were at a very high standard. The salary for a beginning teacher at Sherman was $5,782, which appeared comparable with the Riverside Unified School District salary of $6,420.[40] He noted, however, that the comparability disappeared when it was recognized that Riverside School District salary was for the school year while Sherman salaries were for the entire calendar year. He argued, "This difference could ultimately produce staffs at Sherman Institute which fulfill formal requirements but may lack ability to cope with the special student population" (162).

Svenson found the curriculum in compliance with the requirements of the State of California: "If the basic assumption is accepted that the needs and aspirations of the population served is an academic education leading toward a high school completion certificate, then it follows that the highly structured residential high school environment does indeed accomplish that goal." However, he continued, "If relevancy includes the concept that educational experiences should have the goal of providing students with an awareness of the societies in which they will be called upon to function, substantial gaps exist in the current program" (162).

In June 1969, a conference was held at Sherman Institute under the auspices of Congressman Tunney. Clare J. Taber, Tunney's southern California representative, issued a report on the conference that was as negative as Svenson's. Taber identified the "main crippling factor" as "the lack of necessary financial support." He cited inadequate funding as the cause of a "pervasive negative attitude on the part of the administration and staff" that "has contributed to a stifling atmosphere and has limited the students' performance." Taber perceived a "prevalent prejudgment or expectation that these young people will fail before they even begin." However, he defended the Sherman staff as "generous, hardworking, dedicated people operating under frustrating and extreme handicaps."[41]

Similarly, Svenson found the people at Sherman "doing as good a job as they could with the limitations imposed." In 2011, Dr. Svenson voiced his major criticism of Sherman: "What I observed was a curriculum that was designed to help students get a job right out of high school and not one to prepare students to attend college or university to seek a higher degree leading to one of the professions. With this school culture, the teachers and counselors were not in a position to help students dream a dream and plan their future education to help them realize that dream."[42]

In contrast, Svenson had distinct praise for the California Indian Education Association (CIEA): "Bright, intelligent people were working in the association, which was a stimulus to the power of the Indian people."[43] The CIEA was established in 1968 by David Risling (Hoopa-Karuk and Yurok) and Jack D. Forbes (Powhatan-Renape and Delaware-Renape). The association was the outcome of the first statewide all-Indian conference on Indian education in October 1967 in North Fork, California, home of the North Fork Rancheria of Mono Indians. The ad hoc committee of the North Fork conference stressed increased Indian involvement in the education process, the value of Native heritage, and the restoration of Johnson-O'Malley funds.[44]

When the ad hoc committee evolved into the California Indian Education Association, the CIEA applied the concerns expressed at North Fork to Sherman Institute with these specific recommendations: an all-Indian board of directors, a program that reflected California Indian enrollment, curricula that expressed Indian concepts, a lower student-teacher ratio, and accommodations for visiting parents.[45]

Partly in response to a recommendation by the California Indian Education Association, BIA commissioner Robert L. Bennett announced in a visit to Sherman Institute on January 7, 1967, that California Indians would be enrolled in the school for the first time since 1948. During the visit, Bennett's declarations resonated with self-determination: "A new day is dawning for Indians." He described Indian youths as "young Turks" who were forsaking traditional passive roles and seeking a more active voice in their own affairs, both on and off the reservation. He believed that when the young Turks returned to the reservation, they were influenced by older leaders. "Young Turks and traditionalists alike are being challenged to participate more fully, to voice their opinions and to accept responsibility in tribal affairs, to start helping to solve their own problems." He continued by identifying the responsibility of the federal government to "live up to its commitments, to provide Indians with the vital services that prepared them to assume a full participating share in the complex 20th Century world." He urged Sherman Institute students to utilize education in order to adapt to "the strange new life they find." He declared that Indians must show more awareness and a willingness to live with the consequences of their decisions. He concluded: "I know they can."[46]

Bennett's confidence was echoed by Noel D. Scott, who became superintendent in 1969 and was determined to establish a new image for the renamed Sherman Indian High School. Scott hoped to change the image of Sherman from an institute to that of a high school, the only difference from public high schools being that the students lived at Sherman instead of at home. Despite eight buildings being closed because of earthquake safety requirements, Scott made considerable improvements in the quality of life at Sherman. Portable lighted fountains and stereo music had been installed in the cafeteria. Meals prepared by students enrolled in an institutional cooking class were supplemented by food cooked in an advanced gourmet course.[47] A reporter from the *Riverside Daily Enterprise* described a recent lunch: fried chicken, corn with hominy, mashed potatoes and gravy, hot rolls, cottage cheese, gelatin salad, ice cream, chocolate cake, and milk and coffee, with no limit on the amount eaten.[48] While the menu appealed to the young people, the lack of fruits and vegetables is puzzling given that Sherman's farm supplied ample fresh produce.

Scott articulated his stance: "The policy of self-determination for Indian peoples should be interpreted and implemented at every level. We built it into the curriculum and have real student involvement." Remedial reading showed three years' improvement in one year. Freshmen had an open classroom design, with history, English, and science being taught concurrently, students working individually or in small groups. Absenteeism dropped sharply. Students had a major voice in spending priorities and in drafting and enforcing rules. Harold Nading, principal of Sherman during the early '70s, expressed the change in the administrative policy of Sherman: "When I first came here 99% of the decisions were made for students. They were forced to go to church or even to a movie. They were told what to do, when to do it, and how it was to be done."[49]

During Scott's administration, programs were created to meet the specific needs of students and to give them more responsibility for managing their lives both on and off campus. The programs included a remedial math course with computers, on-the-job occupational training, a physical education program using ultramodern equipment for girls with poor muscular development, and a remedial reading program, cited in a national study by the Department of Education as one of the best in the country.[50]

A notable addition to the Sherman campus, the Sherman Indian Museum, was designed by Superintendent Scott, plant manager Ned T. Robitzer, retired printing instructor Judson M. Bradley, and Ramona Bradley. The museum is housed in the former administration building of Sherman Institute, currently the only original structure remaining on the campus. The museum officially opened on Indian Day, September 25, 1970. The exhibits include the Judson M. Bradley dioramas of California, Plains, Hopi, and Cherokee cultures; the Edith Howard exhibit of Western Plains beaded moccasins; the Oscar B. Colley collection of California Indian baskets; the Don Mason collection of Southwest baskets and California and Plains headdresses; the Peter Grave collection of grass and pine baskets and Mesa Grande pottery ollas; and the Gladys P. Wagner collection of pre-Columbian pottery, including Mimbres, Salado, and Four-Miles polychrome wares.[51]

A major attraction in the museum is the considerable collection of trophies awarded to exceptional athletes of the school. Sherman athletes gained national and international attention, challenging preconceived perceptions about Indians. In addition to exhibits, the museum houses student registration records dating from 1892; issues of the *Sherman Bulletin* from 1907 to the 1980s; and photo archives from 1892 to the present. The museum was designated as a Riverside Cultural Heritage Landmark on October 20, 1974, and was recorded on the National Register of Historic Places on January 9, 1980.[52]

As conditions were improving for Sherman in the late '60s and early '70s, the federal government also was adopting a more positive view of Indian affairs. Richard M. Nixon, who resigned the presidency in disgrace, was nevertheless considered a champion by Indian people.[53] Vice president during the most damaging era of termination, Nixon issued a special message to Congress on July 8, 1970, in which he voiced a stark repudiation of termination: "Because termination is morally and legally unacceptable, because it produces bad practical results, and because the very threat of termination tends to discourage greater self-sufficiency among Indian groups, I am asking Congress to pass a new Concurrent Resolution which would expressly renounce, repudiate, and repeal the termination policy."[54]

He stated in his message to Congress that forced termination had practical results that were "clearly harmful," and the economic and social condition of Indians was often worse after termination than it was before. He also argued that federal termination erred in one direction and federal paternalism erred in the other and called for the advocacy of Indian self-determination, including control of education: "The Federal government needs Indian energies and Indian leadership if its assistance is to be effective in improving the conditions of Indian life. It is a new and balanced relationship between the United States government and the first Americans that is at the heart of our approach to Indian problems. And that is why we now approach these problems with new confidence."

The group most effective in preventing more legislation authorizing terminations was the National Congress of American Indians (NCAI), founded in 1944. Under the leadership of Joseph R. Garry, a Coeur d' Alene, the antitermination campaign of NCAI exemplified the growing commitment of national Indian leaders.[55] Nixon's advocacy of Indian self-determination may have been influenced by the campaign for self-determination that was being waged by Indian activists. With a new spirit of militancy, two hundred Indians occupied the abandoned federal penitentiary on Alcatraz Island in San Francisco Bay. Beginning on November 20, 1969, the occupation lasted for nineteen months, until June 11, 1971, and was the beginning of the Red Power movement.[56]

4

Red Power and Self-Determination

1973-2000

THE OCCUPATION OF ALCATRAZ (1969-71) was of crucial importance in Indian activism. Many of the seventy-four subsequent occupations of federal facilities were planned by people who had been involved in the Alcatraz action. The American Indian Movement (AIM), originally formed to protect urban Indians from civil rights violations, expanded after Alcatraz into multitribal protest activism. In November 1972, AIM took over the BIA headquarters in Washington, D.C., demanding restitution for civil rights violations. The resulting conflict forced the resignation of Commissioner Louis Bruce, the founder of the National Congress of American Indians.[1]

Beginning on February 27, 1973, some two hundred Oglala Lakotas, members of AIM, occupied the town of Wounded Knee on the Pine Ridge Reservation in South Dakota for ten weeks. They attempted to impeach the tribal chairman, Richard Wilson, accusing him of corruption and working too closely with the BIA. The U.S. Marshals Service and FBI agents cordoned off the area, and the conflict became deadly. Two Indians and one FBI agent were killed. As the public became more aware of injustices against Indians, sympathy for the protest grew significantly.[2]

For two days the Sherman High School bulletin board facing Magnolia Avenue displayed the message "Bury My Heart at Wounded Knee." Because of protests by Riverside residents and dissension on campus, the message was taken down, despite a petition to keep it displayed. On March 27, Kathy Guarino, a reporter for the *Arlington Times*, interviewed Sherman students concerning their opinions about Wounded

Knee.³ Many students were unwilling to talk about the occupation, some out of shyness, others because of a feeling of shame caused by the violence. Some expressed strong support for the militants; others voiced fear about the consequences of the violence. Harold Jones, a junior, was supportive of the AIM siege: "It takes something like Wounded Knee to make people understand the Indian, and to make people listen to his needs. Once people know how unhappy the Indian is, maybe they'll do something about the broken treaties."

Cynthia Wyakett, a senior, agreed with Harold in general: "At least people pay attention now," she said. But she was not ready to condone violence. Mike Thom and Joanne Yazzi both disagreed with Jones and Wyakett. Thom feared that the Wounded Knee militants "may have set the Indians back 100 years." He believed education was the means to achieve Indian goals: "The white man only listens to those he respects, those with an education, and most of the militants are dropouts." Yazzi agreed: "A school background is needed to make better homes and better facilities." She was glad, however, that "at least the Indians are speaking up."

Jones and Wyakett perceived white man's education as destructive. Harold Jones said, "The Indian who goes to the white man's public school is nothing. He tries to learn the white man's ways, and even if he does, he can't find a job in the white man's society." Cynthia Wyakett agreed: "The white man's ways are destroying his society. I don't want that for the Indians." All four students expressed appreciation for their education at Sherman. "The tribes want to keep their own ways, their own culture," Wyakett said. "They don't want white man's schools." She also objected to the pressure to take down the message on the bulletin board. "We're all Indians. It's not going to hurt us to stick together. Why can't we put up a sign on our own property?"

When asked what improvements they would like to see in the Bureau of Indian Affairs, Joanne Yazzi wanted more schools like Sherman, and Harold Jones wanted better homes, recreational facilities, and better vocational education. Mike Thom expressed an attitude of self-determination: he wanted nothing from the BIA. "If Indians want to accomplish anything," Thom said, "they'll have to do it for themselves. They have to stop depending on the BIA." Harold thought that the conflict at Wounded Knee would last a long time, and he planned to join the protest that summer. His plans were not realized. The siege ended on May 9, 1973, as the result of negotiations between President Nixon's representative Leonard Garment and AIM leaders Dennis Banks and Carter Camp.

During the subsequent years, numerous occupations of reservations were carried out by AIM members and urban Indians. The last major event of the Red Power movement was the Longest Walk, when several hundred Indians walked February–July 1973 from San Francisco to Washington, D.C., to symbolize the forced removal of Indians from their homelands and call attention to the persisting problems the Indian community faced.[4]

Activism by Indians was recognized with the passage in 1972 of the Indian Education Act, the first major legislative victory in the policy of self-determination. It was an attempt to remedy problems identified in the Kennedy Report and was favorably received by the Indian community, primarily because one of the major provisions was the establishment of the National Advisory Council on Indian Education. The council gave Indians the ability to initiate, implement, and evaluate Indian education programs. The act was limited, though, to public schools.[5] The BIA did start a large building program, including major construction on boarding school campuses. During the tenure of Noel Scott (1969–80), Sherman became an accredited high school and began its critical building program.[6]

Since 1967, students had been attending classes in the dormitories, in a converted laundry facility, and in other rooms serving temporarily as classrooms. When construction began, Ned Robitzer, plant manager for the campus, said, "We have not had a classroom building for the past five years." The first phase of the renovation included an academic center to house science labs, a library and resource center, and classrooms with portable walls and private study cubicles.[7] When the first phase was completed, the construction (with a total cost of $3 million) included remodeled vocational shops in woodworking, metalworking, painting, and drafting; a revitalized athletic field with new bleachers; imposing television and graphic arts equipment; individual cubicles with tape-recorded lectures; and a new library with eight thousand volumes on the shelves and five thousand more on order.[8]

Oliver Green, who was assistant principal in charge of instruction, praised the "efficient planning" of the new complex, especially the open classrooms without walls, which had "stimulated learning." Jim Marion, head of the math and science department, stated that the addition of individual cubicles with tape-recorded instruction "enables the student to progress at his own level." He went on, "It really places the responsibility to learn on the student, and the kids take it very seriously." The Home Economics Department had four new modern kitchens, a banquet room, a fabric store, and a minihospital where child care and nursing were taught in cooperation with Riverside General Hospital. While girls were not allowed to take vocational shop instruction, boys were admitted to the home economics courses.[9]

The driver education lab included thirty individual driver seats, each complete with steering wheel, foot pedals, and an automatic transmission. Operated by a central console, the lab simulated street conditions with students driving in traffic. Sherman also had for the first time two driver education cars. Student reaction to the new atmosphere was especially rewarding to Sherman faculty. "It used to be we had to drag them out of the dorms to get them to come to class," said Vice-Principal Green. "Now we have to kick them out when we close the doors at night. And the kids are really trying to take care of the classrooms, equipment, and carpets. We are really proud of them."[10]

The construction, covering eighty-three acres and providing 185,000 square feet of instructional space, was completed in 1974. "Indian-ness" was avoided in the architecture because of the diversity of Indian tribes represented.[11] The greatly improved physical conditions on the Sherman Indian High School campus were complemented by an administrative policy responding to the campaign for self-determination. The new focus, formally articulating the middle course that students had been negotiating for many years, is stated in the student handbook of 1972–73: "Our school is dedicated to the task of helping each student effectively merge his native culture and his expanding environment."[12]

The policy was evident in the extensive arts and crafts program. "Retaining Indian culture is emphasized. . . . Tribal craftsmen are brought in from the major tribes to teach their specialties." The following sentence, however, raises an unavoidable question: "It is felt that much therapy can be accomplished in such a program and referrals are constantly being made by counselors" (4). Why was therapy needed by students to the degree that "constant referrals" were necessary?

The philosophy of Sherman Indian High School is articulated in this statement in the handbook: "We pride ourselves in achieving student involvement in every phase of campus life. Students are urged to become acquainted with all our services. We truly try to make Sherman a real home away from home for our students" (3). Despite the need for therapy for some students, the rhetoric of the stated philosophy was reinforced by real manifestations of the shift toward self-determination. In addition to a course in Indian history, the course in U.S. and early American history included instruction in the "contributions of American Indians to the development of the American dream as it has grown toward reality" (25).

A more immediate and practical demonstration of self-determination was the Co-educational Honor Dorm, run entirely by students, whose actions are described as follows in the *Handbook*: "They make their own rules, admit students, expel students from the dormitory, and take pride in handling all aspects of home-living" (3). An extension of the Honor Dorm was the Sunset Apartments, built in 1978, giving students the opportunity to become acquainted with independent apartment living. Each apartment had a full furnished living room; a kitchen with stove, refrigerator, dishwasher, and laundry washer and dryer; a bathroom; and a bedroom for two persons. Originally the apartments were intended to be coed like the honor dorm, but this arrangement was not acceptable to parents. One occupant said, "It gives you the feeling of independen[ce,] and you have the privacy you don't have in the dorms."[13] Because of budget cuts, the apartments were closed in 2008.

For three months in 1974, General Motors Corporation was partly owned by twenty students of Sherman Indian High School. Reagan Reed, instructor of a business survey course, realized that his students were not interested in studying stocks and bonds, so he decided to get them directly involved by buying some stock and playing the market. Because the class had no money, the students washed cars for one day, earning $50.[14] The students decided to invest it in General Motors because the company was well-known and because one share cost $50 the day they invested. They followed General Motors stock every day, seeing it rise to $54.[15] When Reed took a vote, the majority decided not to sell, to wait a few weeks. GM sent the students a proxy, and they were able to vote on whether a shareholder should get an extra dividend the next year, whether employees should receive more in retirement funds, and whether GM should consider environmental concerns when making decisions on production. The school year ended on May 22, so the students sold their share on May 3 for $47.[16]

Self-determination has its limits, however. The administration of Sherman Indian High School takes its responsibility very seriously. Under the heading "Social Behavior" in the *Sherman Indian High School Handbook,* good conduct is defined and regulated by school administrators: "Necking, petting, arms around each other, etc., is not permitted on or off campus. Dating privileges will be withdrawn for students who violate the rules" (4–5). One wonders whether students knew what the "etc." referred to. Students were expected to be "clean and WELL-GROOMED at all times" (5).

Other similarly emphasized instructions may indicate administrative experience with student problems: drinking intoxicating beverages, drugs, and sniffing were "ABSOLUTELY" forbidden. If students encountered problems while they were in town, they were advised to inform the staff immediately. "Do NOT attempt to take care of the problem yourself." Under the heading "Other Regulations and Policies," boundary lines beyond which students were not allowed to venture were demarcated: to the south, Barry's Drive-In; to the north, Sherman's front gate; to the east and west, Magnolia Avenue. "To go outside this area, including Riverside," the handbook advised, "a special pass will be needed" (5).

An editorial, "Popping Can Be Permanent," was written in the *Sherman Bulletin* on February 19, 1977, by an unnamed student who seems ambivalent about the abuse of drugs.

> There's been a lot of pill popping in the last few weeks. This may give you a good high, but if you're going to use it, take enough to do some good, not to give you too good of a rush. You may overdo it. Did you ever think of the people you'd be hurting? Your parents care a lot about you. They took the time and energy to raise you. They trust you, that's why they let you go away to school. They

probably know you'd fool around a lot, drinking, smoking and all. Your parents have gone through the same thing. I know other schools have the same problem, but it makes US look worse. The reason for that is because we're Indians. Because we're Indians, we should try harder. We should set an example for others to follow. So let's have a little pride. THINK before you pop.

The impetus toward a major renewal of Sherman Indian High School was clearly evident in its participation in the Model School Project designed by the National Association of Secondary School Principals and supported by the Danforth Foundation between 1969 and 1974. Under the direction of J. Lloyd Trump of the University of Illinois and William Georgiades of the University of Southern California, the project proposed a comprehensive model of school restructuring that was adopted by junior and senior high schools throughout the United States and Canada. The Model School Project promoted a coordinated view of schooling that included changes in the roles of principals, teachers, and students; curriculum revision; and evaluation standards. Sherman was the first BIA school to participate in the project, a unique opportunity to strengthen its educational services and furnish the BIA with a school renewal program for analysis, review, and adaptation by other schools.[17]

Sherman began the Model School Project with emphasis on individual instruction in reading, science, typing, math, and art. An excellent after-school program in recreation and arts and crafts substantially reduced the number of dropouts. A second reading lab was established. The reading lab, supervised by instructor Ruby Shepherd, was selected as a site to be visited as an exemplary compensatory education project, under the Office of Health, Education and Welfare.[18]

Indian education policy reform made major progress during the presidency of Gerald R. Ford, who appointed as commissioners of Indian Affairs Morris Thompson (an Athabaskan from Alaska) from 1973 to 1976 and Benjamin Reifel (a Sioux from the Rosebud Reservation) from 1976 to 1977.[19] On January 4, 1975, Ford signed into law the Indian Self-Determination and Education Assistance Act. Described by President Ford as "a milestone for Indian people," it is considered one of the twentieth century's seminal pieces of federal Indian legislation.

Title II of the act amended the Johnson-O'Malley Act to give the Indian community a stronger role in designing and funding their children's education.[20] In 1979, Noel D. Scott, Sherman's superintendent, stated, "We are looking forward to the implementation of PL 95-561 (Indian Self-Determination and Education Assistance Act) which will provide more Indian Control in Indian education and will result in an Indian school board with full authority and control. There will be less red tape in the areas of personnel, programs, and activities."[21]

The adverse effects of termination and consequent Indian activism initiated a reexamination of federal Indian policy, including its history and the federal government's legal relationship with and responsibilities to Indian people. Congress concluded that federal paternalism had deprived Indians of the opportunity to develop leadership skills and had denied them effective participation in the planning and implementation of programs that were intended to benefit them. Further, Congress found that self-determination was dependent on education, that federal policy had not effected the desired level of educational achievement for Indians, and that parental and community control of education was crucial. Title II of the act established procedures by which tribes could negotiate contracts with the BIA to administer their own educational programs.[22] Sherman Indian High School opened its campus to parents, tribal committees, school boards, and interested members of the public.

Despite these positive developments on the national level, and despite parental involvement, Sherman Indian High School had problems, revealed in surveys reported in the *Sherman Bulletin* on October 17, 1980. Students were asked for their best and their worst impressions of the school. The best impressions included the following comments: "The education is good," "Pretty because of the palm trees," "The girls!" and "The boys!" "You meet a lot of new people and make new friends," and "Going off campus and getting stoned." The worst impressions included, "It's boring," "The food!" "The school has too many requirements," "No fun," "Dirty dorms," "It is smoggy," "Too many fights," "It is dirty," and "Too much smoking pot and drinking."

The last complaint, despite the zero tolerance policy of Sherman, was a significant problem. Fifty students participated in a smoking pot/

drinking poll. Thirty-one admitted to drinking alcohol out of habit or boredom, to forget problems, to have fun, or to socialize. Nineteen smoked pot, likewise out of habit or boredom or to have fun, and also to "freak out." A parents' advisory committee met on campus for two days to deal with their concern regarding drugs and alcohol.[23] In a commemorative video of Sherman's hundredth anniversary, Leroy Miranda, who graduated in 1986, remembered the students' drinking and smoking and couples being "intimate." His wife, Doreen Miranda, who attended Sherman from 1983 to 1986, recalled arriving at Sherman and seeing "kids being wild, running all over campus and climbing in and out of windows." Leroy stated that during his first year at Sherman, students had considerable self-determination and were allowed to stay off campus until midnight, but most of them just walked up and down Magnolia Avenue. During his second year, the curfew was changed from midnight to six o'clock P.M., which "cramped our style with the girls."[24]

Doreen spoke with residual pride about the Utes "sticking together, always fighting with other students." She remembered "jumping the fence, being AWOL from campus, even renting a motel room where school administrators couldn't find us." However, she had meaningful praise for Sherman: "You find out who you are, that you are strong and independent and learning how to adjust to people other than Utes." Both Leroy and Doreen expressed amusing astonishment about one feature of life at Sherman. After emphasizing that they were kids, thirteen to eighteen years old, they exclaimed that students were allowed to drink coffee: "black tar coffee!"[25]

Leroy declared that his days at Sherman were the best time of his life: "You make of this school what you want it to be. If you want the best education, it's available at Sherman. Sherman is one of the best schools anywhere. There are opportunities at this school." Leroy and Doreen expressed taking what they learned at Sherman about themselves and others as Indians back to the reservation at Pala.[26] Their comments reflect the majority of the opinions expressed by Sherman students in a survey taken in 1981 regarding whether Indians who graduate from high school or college should return to the reservation. Those who responded in the affirmative stated that graduates should return to their reservation to teach their people what they had learned and to encourage younger ones to get an education. The minority who responded negatively referred to alcoholism and the lack of good jobs on the reservation. More than one-fourth of the respondents articulated a middle course, believing that if the individual decided independently it would be a good decision.[27]

The development of Indian self-determination, supported by federal policy during the administrations of Presidents John Kennedy, Lyndon Johnson, Richard Nixon, and Gerald Ford was continued by President Jimmy Carter. Forrest Gerard (a member of the Blackfeet tribe of Montana) was the first person to serve in the newly created position of assistant secretary for Indian Affairs of the Interior Department (1977–78). With the assistance of Gerard and his successor, William E. Hallett (a Red Lake Chippewa), Carter was able in 1978 to sign into law the Tribally Controlled Community College Assistance Act and the American Indian Religious Freedom Act.[28]

The self-determination philosophy of Presidents Kennedy, Johnson, Nixon, Ford, and Carter was nominally continued by President Ronald Reagan (1981–89) but was in fact undermined by drastic cuts in funding. Margaret Szasz argues that the Indian policy administered by Reagan and Commissioners Kenneth L. Smith and Ross Swimmer "remains notorious in Indian country." She further contends that Reagan never understood the federal government's legal relationship with Indians, and he declared that Indian education was not a trust responsibility. By the end of Reagan's administration, federal Indian off-reservation boarding schools had been closed, with the exception of four: Sherman Indian High School; Chemawa in Salem, Oregon; Riverside Indian School in Anadarko, Oklahoma; and Flandreau in South Dakota.[29]

Reyhner and Eder provide a detailed discussion of the 1988 *Report on BIA Education*, issued by the Bureau of Indian Affairs, which examined the past and current Indian education policy and effectiveness.[30] Among its findings was the annual turnover rate of more than 20 percent for BIA educational professionals. The BIA had changed its policy from paying higher than average teacher salaries in the 1970s to lower than average in the 1980s. The report concluded that Indian education had some of the best teachers, those who were idealists and reformists, and some of the worst, those who were seeking to escape personal problems with a dramatic change in lifestyle. The pressure to hire Indian teachers often resulted in the hiring of poorly trained ones.

Another problem the report identified was the lack of instruction on Indian history and culture, partly because of the dearth of textbooks and other instructional materials. Because each tribe had its unique history and culture, the market was too limited for mainstream publishers. The report rather naively recommended that specialized material be created locally, perhaps as class projects. Initiated by reports of BIA deception and maladministration, the investigation resulted in disparaging charges: "Paternalistic federal control over American Indians has created a federal bureaucracy ensnarled in red tape and riddled with fraud, mismanagement and waste."[31]

Reagan's policies were mitigated during the administration of George H. W. Bush and Commissioner Eddie Frank Brown, both of whom were in office from 1989 through 1993. Their contributions to Indian self-determination included the Native American Languages Act of 1990 (Public Law 101-477), which made it federal policy "to preserve, protect, and promote the rights and freedom of Native Americans to use, practice, and develop Native American languages." It also recognized "the right of Indian tribes and other Native American governing bodies to use Native American languages as a medium of instruction in all schools funded by the Secretary of the Interior."[32] Other major legislation enacted during the George H. W. Bush administration included the Museum of the American Indian Act, which required the repatriation of Native American artifacts and remains held by the Smithsonian, and the Native American Graves Protection and Repatriation Act (NAGPRA), requiring museums and federal agencies to return Native American human remains and funerary, sacred, and culturally important objects to lineal descendants and affiliated tribes.[33]

Additional support for self-determination was Secretary of Education Lauro F. Cavazos's commissioning of a task force to evaluate American Indian/Alaskan Native education. The final report issued in October 1991, titled *Indian Nations at Risk,* was discouragingly similar to the 1988 *Report on BIA Education.* The criticisms included curricula presented from a Western perspective, ignoring the historical contributions of American Indians and Alaskan Natives; low expectations and Native students performing below basic levels; extremely high dropout rates; teachers with inadequate skills and training; limited library and other learning resources; a lack of opportunities for parental and community involvement; and the loss of Native language ability.

Included in the report was a comprehensive assessment written by Jon Reyhner of the critical dropout rate of Indian students, the highest dropout rate of any ethnic or racial group in the country. Reyhner attributed the problem to the continuing "discontinuity between home and school, forcing Native children to choose between their Native heritage and school success with disastrous results."[34] The report claimed, however, that progress in Indian education had been made since the Kennedy Report was issued in 1969. Some of the progress reported appears tentative: state and local education agencies realized that they had a responsibility to improve the education of Indian students, parents had become more involved in education programs for their children, and some curriculum materials presenting history and culture from a Native perspective had been developed.[35]

In the commemorative video, former student Leroy Miranda spoke highly of Robert Levi, Jr., a Sherman instructor, who presented history from two perspectives, the non-Indian way and what Miranda called "our way." Levi gave him a greatly enhanced interest in history: "I was able to compare histories. While whites were at war, we were living in harmony."[36]

Other progress does appear more promising: the number of Native teachers and administrators in public schools had increased, the number of Native students attending college had increased, and tribally controlled schools and colleges had been developed. Nevertheless, the conclusion of the task force is depressingly redundant: "It is evident that the existing educational systems, whether they be public or federal, have not effectively met the educational, cultural, economic, and social needs of Native communities."[37]

Despite the contributions of the George H. W. Bush administration, Sherman Indian High School administrators and faculty were appreciably disappointed when their expectations were disregarded during a visit to the campus on March 17, 1989, by Secretary of the Interior

Manuel Lujan, Jr., and Secretary of Education Lauro Cavazos. Sherman principal Joe Frazier had requested additional funding of $1.5 million for the school's innovative college preparatory program.[38] The unique program put Sherman students in contact with non-Indian students and classes at colleges and universities in the Riverside and San Bernardino areas. The funds were needed to raise teachers' salaries and to replace budget cuts of $20 per student per year imposed by the Reagan administration.[39]

Frazier objected to the need to obtain grants to fund the college preparatory program and raise teachers' salaries. Assistant Principal Robert Loya was blunt: "We went down the tubes with the Reagan administration, and now we expect nothing from the Bush administration." Officials of the Department of the Interior claimed that visits by two Cabinet members to BIA schools signified a new commitment to Indian education. Secretary Lujan, however, stated that these schools should not expect additional funding in the near future but should work more closely with local public schools. Lujan added, "I don't believe more money necessarily means better education." He continued with awkward advice: "It doesn't cost any more to interact with the Riverside public school system, you know, to exchange teachers, students those things."[40]

Cavazos agreed: "What I like about this place is that there are lots of people contributing in the effort. This is very unique." Sherman teachers earned $8,000 less than teachers in the Riverside public school system.[41] When Lujan was asked whether they should receive higher salaries, he laughed and said, "I think everybody ought to have higher salaries, even me." He expressed surprise at complaints that budget cuts could severely obstruct the continuation of the programs he had come to Sherman to praise: "I'm not sure there have been budget cuts here or there or that there is less money than there was the year before."[42]

These statements angered Sherman teachers, who said that they had been expected to do more with less funding in recent years. Steve Tinling, who had taught mathematics at Sherman for eight years, protested that because of low salaries Sherman had "an enormously high turnover rate of teachers." Additionally, inadequate funding meant deplorable teaching materials, which was made evident by Tinling when he held up a dog-eared algebra book with pages spilling out. Regional BIA officials were more sympathetic to Sherman's needs. Peter Soto, administrator of education programs for the BIA in Phoenix, Arizona (which governed six federally funded schools, including Sherman), stated, "We are cognizant of the fact that we need more money. We are going to have to be resourceful to provide for programs such as those at Sherman."[43]

A manifestation of resourcefulness was evident when the Clarke Behavioral Health Center, funded by the Indian Health Service, was dedicated on the Sherman campus on February 12, 1987. The center was named in honor of Frank Clarke, who graduated from Sherman in 1939 and was one of the first five Indian students to graduate from a U.S. medical school. He served as a Naval Medical Center officer in the South Pacific during World War II and later became a renowned physician working with patients afflicted with substance abuse. He was one of the founders of Indian Students against Drug Dependency (ISADD). Clarke was a strong advocate of combining scientific expertise with "folk medicine" to provide holistic treatment. He reasoned, "Modern medical technology has finally caught up with age-old healing practices of Native medicine men." He believed that the benefits of lodge sweats were proven scientifically and that healing chants were a kind of behavioral modification.[44]

Through the Indian Health Service, he worked as a physician for the Department of Family and Community Medicine at Georgetown University and as a physician at Phoenix Indian Hospital. A Hualapai by birth, he was initiated into a Hopi clan in appreciation of his healing endeavors for Indian people. He received the Distinguished Service Award from the Association of American Indian Physicians.[45] When Sherman established a zero tolerance policy regarding drugs, nicotine, and alcohol, students were expelled after the first offense, and there was no need for a behavioral health center. The center was closed for several years, then reopened in 2007 as the Clarke Cultural Center with the mission to promote Native culture and history to prevent substance abuse. The center is currently without funding but is supported by donations and volunteers from the community, with three part-time staff members: Lorene Sisquoc, cultural traditions director; Josie Montes, home-living assistant; and Jordan McMorris, recreation assistant.[46]

Despite the lack of funding, Sherman's athletic program thrived. During the 1970s and 1980s, Sherman cross-country runners dominated the lower division of the California Interscholastic Federation Southern Section, winning ten championships, including the California State Division III Cross Country title in 1988. The boys' basketball team was unbeaten in the 1989 season of the Pinyon League.

Between 1989 and 1994, the BIA sponsored teams of Indian educators who conducted three-to-four-day examinations of all 184 bureau schools. The appraisals were based on the Effective Schools Monitoring and Evaluation model, developed on attributes that highly effective schools had in common. Information was collected on the policies and procedures of each school regarding written curricula, teaching methods, parental involvement, staff development, and cultural relevance. The evaluations revealed nine areas of strength: safe and supportive environments in 63 percent of the schools; quality instructional leadership, 40 percent; open and caring teachers, 45 percent; high expectations of students, 37 percent; integration of Indian culture, 34 percent; a clean and attractive campus, 33 percent; teachers who were academically qualified, 30 percent; parental involvement, 29 percent; and a school board that was involved and knowledgeable, 19 percent. Ten areas needing improvement were also identified: the need to develop student powers, 40 percent; the need to develop a written curriculum, 42 percent; the need to provide teacher training in current methodology, 40 percent; the need to write a school improvement plan, 38 percent; the need to improve/upgrade school facilities, 36 percent; the need to improve comprehensive needs assessments, 36 percent; the need to write more adequate mission statements, 35 percent; the need to integrate culture into the curriculum, 26 percent; the need to improve counseling services, 22 percent; and the need to upgrade library/media services, 22 percent.[47] The evaluation of Sherman is not included in available documents, but in 1994 Ken Taylor, Sherman's superintendent, testified before the Senate Committee on Indian Affairs in a hearing on the performance of Bureau of Indian Affairs off-reservation boarding schools. Taylor had worked at Sherman for twenty-one years, as a teacher and as the cross-country coach for both boys and girls. The significance of the teams' esteem and affection for

Taylor is expressed in their proclamation of April 30, 2011, that the cross-country course at Sherman would be henceforth known as "Taylor's Trail."[48] Taylor's testimony reflected the areas needing improvement that were identified in the BIA evaluations, but he attributed the defects primarily to inadequate funding:

> I started working at Sherman Indian High School in 1973, and I have gone through the entire administrative system at all levels. I have seen fourteen principals come and go from that school. All of that time, the need for more money was there. . . . I agree that we need to restructure, but the restructuring has to come from within us. We need to involve the total learning community, which starts with the students and works up through the staff, the parents, the unions, the school boards, the tribal people, and the local community. . . . The need for more money will always be there. . . . We must be creative with our budgets. We need to utilize the local resources that are around us, such as the local colleges, junior colleges, the adult education programs, the GED programs, the local service organizations. We must do that.[49]

In 1995 the *Riverside Press-Enterprise* reported the efforts of Taylor to generate support for Sherman from the community. Taylor argued that after more than ninety years in Riverside, Sherman remained an eighty-eight-acre enigma whose students and staff had minimal contact with the community. Sherman's isolation had been largely self-imposed, Taylor said: "The school has traditionally kept to itself, a measure of both the fear of not being accepted and the shyness of reservation children. We have to invite the community in." Riverside Mayor Ron Leveridge responded and visited the school, as did Representative Ken Calvert, state representative of Corona. Following a meeting on the Sherman campus by the Greater Riverside Chamber of Commerce, chamber members revived the Friends of Sherman Indian High School. Additionally, students visited local public schools telling Sherman's story.

When Taylor became superintendent of Sherman Indian High school in 1992, the enrollment was at a record low of 198 students. Taylor's first step to rebuild Sherman's appeal was to visit the leaders of thirty-five Indian tribes in California, New Mexico, Arizona, and

Nevada. By 1995 the school had reached a ten-year high enrollment, and the Western Association of Schools and Colleges (WASC) awarded Sherman a six-year accreditation, the maximum allowed. The president of the Riverside Chamber of Commerce praised Sherman as "a real gem of cultural diversity," adding that bringing Native American heritage to Riverside was significant. "People need to know what an asset they have [in Sherman Indian High School]."[50]

Sherman Indian High School had benefited during the tenure of President Bill Clinton (1993–2001). The American Indian community had sent Clinton a plan for education entitled "Comprehensive Federal Indian Education Policy Statement, A Proposal from Indian Country to the White House." The proposal was incorporated in Clinton's Indian education policy. On March 31, 1994, Clinton signed into law the Goals 2000: Educate America Act, which administered the BIA as a fifty-first state for purposes of funding education. The provisions of the act were very similar to those of the Effective Schools evaluations, and the BIA considered itself one step ahead of Goals 2000 since the bureau had already implemented Effective Schools evaluations and reforms.[51] On August 6, 1998, he issued Executive Order 13096 on American Indian and Alaska Native Education, which set significant goals for Indian students, including proficiency in reading, mathematics, and science; increasing their high school completion, and reducing the negative impact of poverty and substance abuse. As demonstrated in these two acts, Clinton was proactive in Indian affairs, nominating as commissioners Ada Deer (a Menominee) from 1993 to 1997 and Kevin Gover (a Pawnee) from 1997 to 2001. Clinton strengthened the government-to-government relationship between the United States and tribal nations, increased the budget for Indian Affairs, appointed seventy-six Indians to all levels of his administration, campaigned successfully for amendments to strengthen the Religious Freedom Act, and allocated $300 million for BIA schools' construction and repair.[52] The Goals 2000 Act evidently had a positive effect on Sherman Indian High School, which had a graduating class of ninety-three students, the largest in the school's history thus far. A counseling program for at-risk students and an independent study program were credited with the increased graduation rate.[53]

Ada Deer, the first Indian woman to be appointed commissioner of Indian Affairs, approved tribal-state gaming compacts and extended federal recognition to twelve tribes.[54] On September 8, 2000, the 175th anniversary of the Bureau of Indian Affairs, Kevin Gover, on behalf of the bureau, issued a dramatic apology to tribal leaders: "Before looking ahead, this institution must first look back and reflect on what it has wrought and, by doing so, come to know that this is no occasion for celebration, rather it is a time for reflection and contemplation, a time for sorrowful truths to be spoken, a time for contrition. We must reconcile ourselves to the fact that the works of the Agency have at various times profoundly hurt the communities it was meant to serve."[55] As he continued, he spoke of the Trail of Tears, the war for the West, the deliberate spread of disease, and violent death at Sand Creek, on the banks of the Washita River, and at Wounded Knee; the prohibiting of speaking Native languages or conducting religious ceremonies; and making Indian people ashamed of who they were.

He stressed that the worst actions of the BIA were "against the children entrusted to its boarding schools brutalizing them emotionally, psychologically, physically, and spiritually." He stated that he could not speak for the United States but was empowered to speak on behalf of the Bureau of Indian Affairs:

> I extend this formal apology to Indian people for the historical conduct of this agency. . . . We cannot ask your forgiveness, not while the agency's history weighs so heavily on tribal communities. What we do ask is that together we allow the healing to begin. . . . Tell your children that time of shame and fear is over. Tell your young men and women to replace their anger with hope and love for their people. Together, we must wipe the tears of seven generations. Together we must allow our broken hearts to mend. Together we must face a challenging world with confidence and trust. Together let us resolve that when our future leaders gather to discuss the history of this institution, it will be time to celebrate the rebirth of joy, freedom, and progress for the Indian nations.

An additional apology from the White House was pursued during the "Reconciliation Tour" organized by White Bison, a nonprofit group devoted to helping Indian communities and individuals in need of healing. The cross-country tour visited Sherman Indian High School in May 2009. Don Coyhis, president of the Colorado-based White Bison organization, said that the high alcoholism and suicide rates among Indian people were due in part to the legacy of "trauma caused by the boarding schools." He added, however, that Indians would never be free of the trauma unless they forgave the oppressors: "The first step is forgiveness. Then the healing starts." He asserted that Indians would forgive those who oppressed Indian children even if President Barack Obama did not issue an apology.[56]

President Obama (2009–) did approve "an apology to Native Peoples of the United States" that unfortunately was buried in the 2010 defense appropriations bill. It has been a little-noticed expression of regret for how the federal government misused its power. The language of the apology states, in part, that "the United States, acting through Congress, recognizes that there have been years of official depredations, ill-conceived policies, and the breaking of covenants by the Federal government regarding Indian Tribes." The apology concludes with a commitment "to move toward a brighter future where all the people of this land live reconciled as brothers and sisters, and harmoniously steward and protect this land together."[57]

Navajo students in the special five-year program, which began in 1946.

Boys working on the Sherman ranch, 1930s.

Girls working on the Sherman ranch, 1940s.

The outing system, begun in 1893 at Perris Indian School, continued at Sherman until 1930.

Sherman campus bakery, site of training for institutional baking and cooking.

Boys making bread in the campus bakery, 1930s.

Sherman girls in the Rural Home Life course, which included child care, 1930s.

Student mechanics working on the ranch machinery, 1946.

Boys doing carpentry, 1940s.

The Sherman Band performed at football games, campus concerts, and community parades.

Classroom in 1963, when Sherman had resumed a regular high school program after the Special Navajo Program ended.

Harold Nading, Sherman administrator from 1962 to 1975.

Roland Doepner, English teacher at Sherman Indian High School from 1992 to 1995 and principal since 2008.

Lorene Sisquoc, cultural traditions director and curator of Sherman Indian Museum, circa 2000.

5

Self-Determination and At-Risk Students

2001–2012

KEVIN GOVER'S APOLOGY WAS DRAMATIC RHETORIC, and far more public than Obama's, but it was not converted into action during the administration of President George W. Bush (2001–2009), who was not proactive in Indian affairs. Bush reassured Indians of the government-to-government relationship but believed that states' rights had priority over tribal rights. During his administration, he appointed seven different commissioners of Indian Affairs, four of them acting. His first commissioner, Neal A. McCaleb (2001–2003), a Chickasaw, resigned after he and Interior Secretary Gale Norton were found in contempt of court for mismanagement of tribal trust funds.[1] David W. Anderson (2004–2005), a Choctaw/Ojibwe, resigned following a conflict-of-interest controversy regarding his investment in Indian gambling.[2] The resignation of Carl J. Artman (2007–2008), an Oneida, was reputed to be the result of conflicts in the Interior Department.[3]

David W. Anderson, who was assistant secretary of the Interior for Indian Affairs (2004–2005), was the founder of the Famous Dave's of America restaurant chain. Highly sought after as a keynote speaker, he shared his philosophy based on his life story of overcoming critical obstacles. He visited Sherman Indian High School in March 2004 with his message about positive thinking: "Sherman students face incredible personal challenges that I, myself, have faced. I want to impress upon them what I have learned: positive thinking and healthy life choices can empower anyone to build a life based on hope for a better future."[4]

Of more immediate and practical assistance to Sherman students was the $1 million grant, part of $4 million awarded by the Maxwell

H. Gluck Foundation to the University of California–Riverside to fund outreach in the arts to partner institutions, including Sherman Indian High School. Workshops in 2004 included dancers, choreographers, singers, actors, poets, and art historians, teaching and performing for students who had no other access to instruction in these arts.[5]

The G. W. Bush administration had a major impact on American education, including Indian schools, with the passage of Executive Order 13336, the No Child Left Behind (NCLB) legislation, a reauthorization of the Elementary and Secondary Education Act. In a memorandum to heads of executive branch departments and agencies on September 23, 2004, Bush stated that with this executive order he reiterated his administration's adherence to tribal sovereignty and self-determination.[6] The act required schools to show adequate yearly progress in closing the achievement gap between Indian and white mainstream students. Failing to do so would result in a variety of penalties, including the possibility of termination of employment. Progress was measured by standardized tests.[7]

As the act's effects began to surface, they created considerable controversy, with many educators and policy makers doubting the feasibility and fairness of its goals and time constraints. Grave concerns arose, particularly regarding the directives related to adequate yearly progress. In 2006, 29 percent of schools nationwide were failing to achieve adequate yearly progress, and the percentage of failing schools rose to 38 percent by 2010. NCLB did, however, have advocates expressing support for stringent accountability and transparency of results.[8]

Jon Reyhner reported in 2006 that many schools were failing to show adequate yearly progress of Indian students: "Educators and parents are desperately looking for ways to increase their students' test scores, which often means narrowing the curriculum to just prepare the students for the reading and mathematics tests required by NCLB." He argued that while the Indian education provisions of NCLB gave lip service to the importance of culture-based education, NCLB was creating a one-size-fits-all curriculum on reading and math, while history and the arts were nearly abandoned. "This test preparation curriculum hinders teachers trying to connect education to the lives of students in their communities with the result that schooling is becoming increasingly boring and disconnected from student lives."[9]

The National Indian Education Association (NIEA) was even more critical of No Child Left Behind. David Beaulieu, president of the NIEA, stated, "We are facing a crisis in Indian Education." The NIEA report on the legislation found that the few successes of NCLB had been at the expense of Native languages and cultures, and Indian children were internalizing the failures of No Child Left Behind as their own personal failures.[10]

An act more favorable for Indian students, the Esther Martinez Native Languages Preservation Act, was signed into law by President Bush on December 14, 2006.[11] The bill authorized funding for new programs to prevent the loss of Indian languages and cultures. The act was named in honor of Esther Martinez, a language teacher from New Mexico, as a tribute to her efforts to preserve the Tewa language. Passage of the act required intense lobbying by the National Alliance to Save Native Languages, which argued that of the more than 300 Native languages spoken at the time of contact in the United States, only 175 remain. The prediction was that unless efforts were made to teach the languages to new generations, by 2050 only 20 will survive. The National Indian Education Association enlisted the help of the Navajo Code Talkers to lobby for the act.[12]

President Barack Obama (2009–) offered relief from some of the mandates of the No Child Left Behind Act when he authorized waivers in February 2012 to ten states that had submitted substantial school reform plans to the Department of Education. The waiver plan, which does not require congressional approval, is part of Obama's "we can't wait" series of executive orders. Thirty-eight states, including California, and the District of Washington had submitted requests by May 2012. "The best ideas to meet the needs of individual students are going to come from the local level," said Arne Duncan, secretary of Education. "These plans will protect children, raise the bar and give states the freedom to implement reforms that improve student achievement."[13]

President Obama and Larry Echo Hawk (a Pawnee), assistant secretary of the Interior for Indian Affairs,[14] designed a 2010 budget that decreased funds for Indian Affairs overall but increased funding by $8.9 million for Indian education. On February 25, 2010, Echo Hawk stated in testimony before the Senate Committee on Indian Affairs, "One of our top priorities is to improve Indian education and provide quality educational opportunities to Native American students." On December 2, 2011, the president issued an executive order, titled "Improving American Indian and Alaska Native Education Opportunities and Strengthening Tribal Colleges and Universities." The order states, in part, "It is the policy of my administration to support activities that will strengthen the Nation by expanding educational opportunities and improving educational outcomes for all AI/AN students in order to fulfill our commitment to furthering tribal self-determination and to help ensure that AI/AN students have an opportunity to learn their Native languages and histories and receive complete and competitive education that prepares them for college, careers, and productive and satisfying lives."[15]

Despite the well-meaning intentions of the Obama administration and the executive order to support them, Sherman Indian High School had to cope with cuts that were described as devastating. In February 2009, the school was forced to lay off thirty-four employees, including three teachers, eight teacher aides, one psychologist, one social worker, three administrative employees, and eighteen dorm staff. The layoffs resulted in the teaching staff being reduced to twenty instructors for 363 students. The remaining teachers were required to teach more courses and assume the work of the laid-off teacher aides. Three dorms were closed, and students were crowded into the remaining five: Wigwam and Kiva for the boys and Dawaki, Ramona, and Winona for the girls. In October 2011, thirty more employees lost their jobs at Sherman. The laid-off staff included food-service workers, clerks, secretaries, a counselor, an accountant, six teacher aides, and the vice principal, Carl Davis.[16]

In the budget for 2013, the funds for Indian education were increased $653,000, but none of the increase was targeted for off-reservation boarding schools. Federal Indian boarding school budgets are based on year-round enrollment, and Sherman's enrollment had dropped from 640 in 2006–07 to 452 in 2010–11 and 350 in 2011–12.[17] Because of personal, family, or tribal problems, Sherman students may have to return home before completing the school year. Also, for many it is the first experience away from home. Leaving a small town or reservation and arriving in Riverside, with a population of 300,000 and an hour's drive from the major urban area of Los Angeles, can be intimidating. The care and nurturing of the young Indians attending Sherman Indian High School is an immense, complex responsibility. Achieving a balance between self-determination for the students and the staff's responsibilities toward them can be challenging.[18]

The Philosophy Statement expressed in the *Sherman Indian High School Student Guide to Success* clearly recognizes the need for a degree of self-determination, while also acknowledging the complexity of the school's mission: "Through shared decision-making, the students, staff, parents, school board, and community of SHERMAN INDIAN HIGH SCHOOL will provide a safe, caring environment in which a balanced program will foster academic, social, cultural, physical, and spiritual growth of a diverse population of AMERICAN INDIANS in an off-reservation boarding school for post-secondary success." The virtuous Vision Statement on the same page of the *Student Guide* also emphasizes shared self-determination: "And to this end we will cultivate and sustain a learning community (to include all staff, students, parents, guardians, tribal leaders, educational coordinator, and board members) dedicated to continuous learning and renewal through self-improvement and assessment, recommitment and collegial support."[19]

The Philosophy and Vision Statements are followed by a letter signed by the four board members: President Raymond Lopez, who is a member-at-large; Vice President Ivan "Rocky" Whitman, from Gila River Indian Community in Arizona; and Marilynn King-Johnson and Garfield Apple, both Oglala Sioux. The Sherman Indian High School Board is distinct evidence of a self-determination policy dramatically different from the policies of Thomas Jefferson Morgan and Richard Pratt, who designed the assimilation model used by Sherman administrators for many years. However, an indication that the administration of an off-reservation school is in some ways more difficult recently than in earlier years is revealed in this sentence by the board of trustees in the *Sherman Indian High School Student Guide to Success*: "As a Board we have worked closely with the Administration and Line Office [of the Bureau of Indian Education] to provide intervention, whenever appropriate for students with substance or disciplinary issues."[20]

Although studies consistently show that Indian students are at greater risk than non-Indians, hazardous behavior by Indians is not unique. One study shows 50 percent of BIA students being current drinkers, with 39 percent of them engaging in heavy episodic drinking; 56 percent were current smokers; and 50 percent were using marijuana.[21] Another study shows that 42 percent of students in the general population were current drinkers, with 24 percent being binge drinkers; 20 percent were smokers; and 7 percent were marijuana users.[22] Although the rate of at-risk behavior for Indians is higher, the evidence shows that it is a significant nationwide problem among students generally. Suicide is the second leading cause of death among Indian youths and is the third leading cause of death for young people in the general population.[23] Substance abuse is frequently a component of suicide.

Amy Bergstrom, Linda M. Cleary, and Thomas D. Peacock interviewed 120 Indian students in depth regarding substance abuse; their study results are published in *The Seventh Generation: Native Students Speak about Finding the Good Path*. Not surprisingly, these students identified the following preventative measures: good connections to parents, the community, teachers, and schools.[24] The Sherman administration has made impressive efforts to maintain these connections, fulfill their responsibilities, and allow a realistic degree of self-determination.

In the *Sherman Indian High School Student Guide to Success,* twenty-two of the fifty pages are devoted to specific disciplinary issues, from minor to major and even expellable. The restrictions, evidently essential in contemporary Sherman life, are sometimes reminiscent of the military regulations of earlier years: Being AWOL is a major violation. Students who leave campus must do so with adult supervision. Guilt by association, knowingly participating in a violation taking place, which may include simply being present, is also a major act of disobedience.[25] The dress code is specifically restrictive. Among items that are not allowed are hoods worn inside or outside in good weather and either red or blue t-shirts, which are evidently gang associated; other disallowed items include sunglasses worn indoors, muscle shirts, and hats, bandannas, beanies, and do-rags (head covering of stretch material made to fit like skull caps).[26] There are so-called daily flight checks (DFCs) for students who are having difficulty of any kind in class, by which each of the student's teachers records his or her observations on a daily basis on the DFC forms.[27]

Minor violations result in demerits, which must be worked off in the student's dorm. There is no explanation as to how this process works. Major violations include misuse of electronic resources, bullying (which has a half page of definitions and examples), harassment, intimidation, hate violence, continual disruptive behavior, cheating, plagiarism, forgery, fighting (except in self-defense), possession of paraphernalia associated with drugs (including alcohol) and with smoking and tattooing, refusal of testing, sexual misconduct, theft or shoplifting, truancy, vandalism, and continued defiance of authority. A major disciplinary referral will result in a meeting with the dean of discipline, documentation of the misbehavior sent to the student's parents or guardians, and an assignment to the Choice Program.[28]

Sherman established the Choice Program to provide additional structure and intervention for students who have committed a major violation of school policy. Students who commit one major violation are automatically referred to the program for a minimum of seven days. While in the Choice Program, students must attend classes and complete assigned academic work but are not allowed to participate in athletics, social events, clubs, fundraisers, and dances, or receive food delivery from off campus or spend time in the quad or the Student Center. Choice Dorm students are escorted to meals. CDs, stereos, iPods, radios, cell phones, and any other electronic equipment are not allowed.[29]

There are additional behaviors that warrant intervention but still may result in being expelled from the school. These include being AWOL or off-campus after midnight; drinking or possessing alcohol; vandalizing property; possessing a weapon; committing felonies such as arson, assault or battery, and sexual assault, as well as issuing bomb threats and being in possession of drugs; participating in gang-related activities; hazing; bullying at a level offensive enough to be declared criminal; misusing print, image, video, or audio equipment in a way that causes damage to the reputation of the school or the government; and using government property without authorization.[30] Every student is entitled to due process in every instance of disciplinary action for alleged violation of school regulations. Students have the right to appeal a disciplinary referral, which provides the opportunity to explain the misconduct and why the student believes the incident should not have resulted in a disciplinary referral. The appeal process is well-defined and may result in the dismissal of the disciplinary referral, reflecting a degree of self-determination.[31]

Zero tolerance behaviors are using/possessing alcohol and/or drugs, participating in gang-related activities, huffing or snuffing any substance, refusing the Choice Program, refusing the substance abuse test, and having five or more major violations. The zero tolerance policy was adopted in 2004, with continuation of the policy being approved by the school board in 2008. The policy has been modified, however. The school board acknowledges the profound negative effects that alcohol and drug use have at the individual, family, tribal, and community level, particularly among youths, and the board recommended in the spring of 2009 that the school site consider approaches toward addressing first-time drug and alcohol offenses that allow a measure of self-determination.[32]

In an effort to provide support for at-risk students, Sherman has instituted intervention procedures for first-time violators of zero tolerance behaviors. These students may be allowed to stay on campus if they agree, with parental or guardian support, to begin an intervention program. The student will sign a contract regarding the terms of the intervention; complete daily flight checks for a specified number of days; attend meetings such as Alcoholics Anonymous, Narcotics Anonymous, or counseling (as required); and being subject to searches or tests throughout the remaining school year and the following fall semester. On-site licensed mental health professionals—including psychologists, clinical social workers, and a psychiatrist—are available from the Indian Health Service, as needed. If there are no violations during this time, students may continue their education without the restrictions of intervention.[33]

In addition to students with alcohol and/or drug problems, others who would not be admitted to Sherman Indian High School in the past because of previous difficulties in school situations are now allowed to attend Sherman on a probationary basis. Those who complete the academic year successfully are allowed to return the following year without probation. The Intensive Residential Guidance (IRG) Program is provided during specified periods in the dormitories and is mandatory for designated students needing help in personal development and life skills. The objectives of IRG are to reduce or end disruptive behavior, improve individual self-discipline and good choice making, channel leisure time toward positive activities, assist students in being responsible for their actions, create an awareness of contemporary careers, prevent chemical and substance abuse, improve social skills, increase classroom attendance, assist students in achievement, motivate and assist students to improve grades to a minimum of C in each class, and motivate students to participate in school activities. Although IRG has not been singularly funded for several years, it has been integrated into the general residential (Homeliving) funding at Sherman. An IRG hour is available at least four nights per week, during which programs may include tutoring and/or counseling.[34]

Activities available include the Athletic Program, offering baseball, boys and girls basketball, boys and girls cross-country, football, boys and girls track and field, and girls volleyball and softball. Girls may also participate in football and baseball. Sherman Indian High School is a member of the California Interscholastic Federation, Southern Section. Sherman also has an intensive intramural program with an Olympic-size indoor swimming pool, a gymnasium with a capacity of over two thousand, a large weight room, lighted tennis courts, handball courts, a lighted football field, outdoor basketball courts, softball and baseball fields, a grass volleyball court, a quarter-mile track, a jogging trail, pool tables, and even poker and domino tournaments.[35]

Complementing the sports program are a variety of clubs, one devoted to each class (freshman through senior) and one for each dorm. Others include the annual Pow Wow, which was started in 1986 by Tonita Largo and Victor Begay. Students may participate in drum, dance, Miss Sherman, spiritual activities, yearbook, and skaters (for skateboard riders, a favorite Native pastime).[36] The Rec Council is maintained by students who like to plan recreational activities. The student governing power is the Inter-Tribal Council, which plans and implements campuswide activities and events throughout the year, including pep rallies, spirit week, homecoming events, dances, movies, the Miss Sherman Pageant, and the annual Pow Wow. Recreation in the Student Center includes movies, tennis, and pool tournaments.[37] The Sherman Indian High School Marine Cadets, participants in the Marine Corps Junior ROTC, study Marine Corps history and the military customs of the country, have close order drills, and participate in community outreach, including appreciation activities in honor of Riverside military veterans.

Independent study is offered to students who are behind in courses needed to graduate. In addition to these administrative programs for students who need support, the Student Study Team (SST)—a program devised and supervised by students—is also available and relies on self-determination. The SST meets to discuss the academic problems of students who have been referred by teachers, staff, or parents or through self-referral. Members of the committee carefully assess the student's needs, share available information, and recommend a plan for assistance, which is directed to the literacy educational specialist.[38]

An effective program to combat drug and alcohol abuse and unsafe sexual behavior is STAND (Students Together Against Negative Decisions), which also relies on self-determination. Sherman was selected by the BIE in 2009 as a pilot site for STAND, which relies on peer counselors trained in the prevention of pregnancy, HIV/AIDS and other sexually transmitted diseases, and drug and alcohol abuse and dating violence. Multifaceted presentations focus on personal development, self-esteem, diversity, goals, values, decision making, negotiation, and refusal skills. The student counselors assist their peers in making healthy decisions by providing comprehensive information about these potentially destructive issues. The program was still in effect at Sherman in 2012 with full-campus presentations and smaller forums with dorm groups that are sponsored by the San Bernardino and Riverside County Indian Health Services. A critical component of the STAND program is embracing the power of traditional teachings and cultural strengths.[39]

In addition to the many intervention programs, Sherman has a twelve-page Holistic Health Program, which is a mental health crisis protocol. It includes assessing the potential for a student harming self or others and for the probability of suicide. Sherman students who are at risk for a mental health crisis, for alcohol or substance abuse, or for academic problems are offered exceptional opportunities to surmount their difficulties and complete an excellent educational program, which has enhanced its academic resources dramatically within the past few years.[40]

Roland "Tripp" Doepner became principal of Sherman Indian High School in 2008. He had previously (1992–1995) taught English at the school, establishing Advanced Placement English courses and an English as a Second Language program. His focus is on preparing students for higher education and the demands of increasingly technological employment.[41] Sherman has a standard high school academic program, but students from so many diverse cultures and experiences present unique challenges. Some students arrive at Sherman with disparities in reading, writing, and math. One of the most effective methods for helping students improve significantly is the Accelerated Reading Program, which includes dedicated reading time, after-class support, and study groups. Learning time is built into the residential program with study groups and workshops in the dorms.[42]

Because many students have to return home before completing the school year, their academic progress is slower than that of typical high school students. Their Native communities, geographically distant from classes or tutoring, may not be able to provide academic support. With current technology, however, remote reservations now have access to online resources. Off-reservation boarding schools are exploring the feasibility of distance learning via the Internet, which would help minimize the interruption in education.[43] Being in residence at the high school, however, offers considerable advantages that cannot be simulated in distance learning.

One of the most significant opportunities in the history of Sherman Indian High School was presented on May 13, 2010, when the San Manuel Band of Serrano Mission Indians announced a commitment of $2.5 million for a Career Technical Education Program at the school. The San Manuel Band, a federally recognized tribe, is located near the city of Highland, California. The Serrano Indians are the Indigenous people of the San Bernardino mountains and valleys who share a common language and culture. Their remarkable gift to Sherman Indian High School is one of many manifestations of their spirit of giving.[44]

A unique partnership of tribal, school, and county associations was formed to create career pathways that will lead to new employment options for students and economic development in Native communities. The program is administered by the Riverside County Office of Education in cooperation with the San Manuel Band and the Sherman Indian Foundation, dedicated to fiscal and resource support for Sherman Indian High School.[45]

During the announcement ceremony, Kenneth M. Young, Riverside County superintendent of schools, thanked the San Manuel Band for supporting education, adding, "This program fits with our pledge to help all students become academically successful, graduate, and be prepared for college and the workforce." James Ramos, chairman of the San Manuel Band, said, "Native peoples on the whole face disparities in health, employment and community development. It is our hope that the pathways set out through this partnership will enable these students to make a brighter future through increased employment opportunities." Ray Lopez, president of Sherman Indian Foundation, described the Career Technical Education Program as a "blessing." He praised the San Manuel Band for understanding the importance of vocational education as a component in the overall Sherman experience and added, "We will do our part to make sure we fulfill the promise of this partnership."[46]

The program includes state-approved courses that meet requirements for graduation and training in five career pathways: health sciences, public services, hospitality in tourism and recreation, agricultural and natural resources, and energy and utilities. The latter component, begun in the fall of 2010, prepares students in the emerging renewal energy industry. Sherman's 2011 valedictorian, Unique Darrell, decided on a health career after taking career pathways courses: "We learned about a lot of medical careers and now I want to be an ultrasound technician. It will really be a help to my community." Graduates in Unique's class included eighteen students with twenty-two Career Technical Education certificates in addition to high school diplomas. The partnership has plans to expand the program to other career options.[47]

Sherman students who have had training in institutional culinary work, particularly the boys, have been able to secure good jobs on cruise ships and in resorts and hotels. The San Manuel Band has provided funds for the culinary arts career pathway and in 2012 funded a completely remodeled Culinary Arts Kitchen Lab. Principal Roland Doepner stated, "Students who wish to earn certificates in food preparation, safety, and nutrition have the opportunity to prepare for high-level careers in restaurant and resort businesses."[48]

Other supportive funding has been donated by the Giving Program of the Pala Band of Mission Indians, which has provided funds to Sherman Indian High School for annual sports banquets. The Pala Band of Mission Indians in northern San Diego County lives on a 12,273-acre reservation, established for Cupeño and Luiseño Indians, who considered themselves one Indigenous people.[49]

In 2010 Edison International provided funds to enable Sherman students to receive tutoring from California Baptist University (CBU). Three CBU faculty members and twelve CBU students provide eighty hours of tutoring a week, specialized assistance in algebra, precalculus, chemistry, and physics. Dr. Anthony Donaldson, dean of the CBU School of Engineering, believes that the participation of CBU in the program is more than academic tutoring: "Our faculty and students recognize the opportunity they have to help these high school students succeed in school and live their purpose."[50]

In 2011 Edison donated another $25,000 to the Sherman Indian High School Career Partnership with the Riverside County Office of Education. This grant is used to support employment preparation and internships for students who are enrolled in the Energy and Utilities Pathway. Students in this pathway are instructed on basic principles of electronic circuitry, the nature of light sources, light amplification, and the integration of optical systems with electronic systems. Sherman students use prototype models that allow them to capture and convert energy from wind and solar sources for power management.[51]

In the fall of 2011, Sherman Indian High School expanded its course offerings to include five major career pathways: Health Sciences; Public Service and First Responders (Firefighting, Paramedic Services, Law Enforcement); Hospitality, Tourism, and Recreation (Culinary Arts with Certifications); Alternative Energy and Utilities and Natural Resource Management; and Bio-Agricultural Science. Each pathway includes industry, state, or national certification; students who choose to enter the workplace upon graduating or want to work while attending college will have a strong competitive advantage.[52]

Sherman participates in the Eligibility in Local Context Program (ELC) through the University of California. To be considered for ELC, students must complete eleven specific subject requirements by the end of the junior year: one year of history/social science, three years of English, two years of mathematics, one year of laboratory science, one year of language other than English, and three years selected from other "a-g" requirements. Fully eligible ELC students are guaranteed a spot at one of the UC undergraduate campuses, although not necessarily their first choice. Students must also submit scores from either the SAT Reasoning test or the ACT Plus Writing test. For some colleges, the SAT Subject tests are also required. A student who is a graduate of any school in California operated by the BIA, including Sherman, is entitled to residence classification for a California college, which allows them the same tuition rate as California residents.[53]

Sherman students have participated in an additional career pathway by joining the Pomona Health Career Ladder of the Western University of Health Sciences. As a cohort of the Pomona program, Sherman students are known as the American Indian Health Ladder, receiving practical medical skills such as using stethoscopes and reflex hammers and taking blood pressures, with the goal of assisting in community health screening. Elizabeth Rega, associate professor of osteopathic medicine at Western University, believes that Sherman students will have their imaginations stimulated and their horizons expanded: "We are really trying to prepare them for being community health ambassadors. This is a good way to do it."[54]

Another group that finds special satisfaction in helping Sherman Indian High School is the Southern California College of Optometry (SCCO) in partnership with Little Eagle Free, Inc., an organization dedicated to assisting Indians in developing productive lives through educational programs. Optometric interns and faculty from the college of optometry provided comprehensive eye examinations to Sherman High School students and assisted them with selecting eyeglass frames on Vision Care Day, December 10, 2010. Little Eagle Free contributed funds for frames and lenses. Established in 1904, the Southern California College of Optometry is a private, nonprofit educational institution, with an outreach clinical program, with many of its sites on Indian reservations.[55]

Vision Care Day was the idea of Frances Knott, board of trustee chair of SCCO and also the founder and chair of Little Eagle Free. She has Choctaw heritage from both parents and is a voting member of the Choctaw Nation of Oklahoma. Watching the Sherman students selecting frames, she said, "It does my heart good to be part of this process. It's good for me to directly help these young people. Giving back is part of my culture. We believe in the importance of family and community, respect for all living things, the bonding of one generation to another and the responsibility for the care and nurturing of our children"[56]

The students who were interviewed for *The Seventh Generation* also spoke about the significance of tribal, cultural, and personal characteristics and resources.[57] In the literature on preventing and treating risky behavior, one essential factor consistently appears: reliance on Indian traditions. Indian students have been exposed to traditional ethics in their home communities, and Sherman staff members remind them of these traditions. In the Talking Circle Room, for example, are displayed pictures of Indians in traditional dress, celebrating events such as coming-of-age ceremonies and weddings. The gathering of plants in Southern California by students for basket weaving is an important aspect of learning to heal the community and heal the earth. Students are taught that drug abuse is not their tradition. They are encouraged to become involved in the traditions, the tribal government, and the ceremonies of Sherman and to continue their involvement in their home communities.[58]

Unlike in the past, the use of Native languages is encouraged, and Fern Charley-Baugus teaches a course entitled Diné Bizaad, that is, Navajo language and culture. The Sherman Indian Museum, the Clarke Culture Center, and the Native Traditions Classroom have language books and audio recordings to help students stay connected to their tribal communities.[59] Marianna Taylor, who had taught English for twenty-nine years at Sherman before retiring in 2001, was encouraged in the 1970s by a Pawnee student to create a course in Native American literature. She believes that courses in Native culture make a student whole. She praised Sherman students for taking the best from both white and Indian cultures.[60]

The Native literature course was the kernel, which was expanded into a Native culture program by Charley-Baugus and Sisquoc, who endeavor to revive deep-rooted Native traditions, such as basket weaving. Students work, for example, on splitting, cleaning, and preparing reeds that were picked on the nearby Cahuilla Reservation. One class made a round-reed, creek-side basket, a two-wall Cherokee basket, a twined flicker bird trap, and a basket rattle. Sisquoc illuminates the multicultural similarities and differences through the form and function of baskets and explains the meanings of animal depictions and symbols in relation to oral traditions. Students accompanied by instructors gather willow from the Santa Ana River to build sweat lodges.

Ongoing traditional activities under the supervision of Sisquoc include the "talking circle," a traditional Native American ritual that is open to all students who need support. After being cleansed and blessed, the Eagle Feather, which is used to communicate truth and prayer, is passed to each participant, when he or she voluntarily speaks. Other Native traditions at Sherman include Sacred Voices speaker series, Pow Wow workshops, and intertribal dance group performances. Sisquoc finds a contradiction in her teaching Native arts at Sherman, regretting that they are not taught in the students' families. She explains that Native traditions are now taught in boarding schools because, ironically, boarding schools in the past suppressed all expressions of these traditions, and generations of students who did not learn the old ways could not pass them on.

A significant advantage for Sherman's students is that they not only acquire a deeper connection with their own culture but also learn about the many other Indian cultures of their peers.[61] In 2012, sixty-eight tribal affiliations were represented by Sherman students, the largest three being seventy-nine Navajos from four different agencies, forty-four White Mountain Apaches, and thirty-seven from the Tohono O'odham Nation.[62]

As in the past, students from the same tribe will form bonds and support groups, but they also have opportunities to learn about other Indian cultures. Leroy Miranda, a Cupeño, who graduated from Sherman in 1986, was amazed to see so many Indians at the school. He stated, "When I first came to Sherman all the Indians looked alike." Gradually, over time, he could easily distinguish the tribal affiliation of individual students. There were no other students from his Southern California Cupa reservation at the time, so he hung out with students from Rincon and La Jolla, geographically close and culturally similar. He also bonded with Hopis and Utes, and he married a Ute woman he met at Sherman. Leroy had attended a public school before enrolling in Sherman and remembers that Indian students were stereotyped as troublemakers and there was considerable tension in the school. "I've learned so many things that I wouldn't have learned in a non-Indian school. Although each tribe has its own culture, we have a common bond."[63]

Despite these significant changes in off-reservation boarding schools, contemporary Indian students drop out for reasons similar to those in earlier years. The literature on Indian student dropout rates is extensive; particularly notable is work by Jon Reyhner, who explored the issues of American Indian/Alaska Native education for the Indian Nations at Risk Task Force in 1992. He identified major problems and offered suggested solutions: restructure large schools, replace uncaring teachers and counselors with Indian personnel, convert passive instruction into interactive methods, use culturally relevant teaching materials, and increase parental involvement to reduce cultural discontinuity.[64]

Susan Ledlow in an article in the *Journal of American Indian Education* in 1992 argued that although much literature on American Indian dropouts accepted cultural discontinuity as an explanation for the high rates, there was little research to support the conclusion. She maintained that economics and social structure may be more important factors.[65] Richard St. Germaine summarized the literature on dropout rates of Indian students dating to 1996, then concluded that cultural discontinuity is one of the obstacles Indian students face in completing their high school education, but it is not the only one. He identifies poverty as a significant cause of high dropout and low graduation rates.[66] Susan C. Faircloth and John W. Tippeconnic III, working for the Civil Rights Project of UCLA, in 2010, examined the graduation and dropout rates among American Indian and Alaskan Native students using data from the National Center for Education Statistics and concluded that these statistics show the rates to be of "urgent concern."[67]

Twenty years before Reyhner made his recommendations in the *Indian Nations at Risk* report, Sherman had implemented several of them. Restructured features of the eighty-eight-acre campus—including the modernized vocational shops, the driver's education lab, individualized cubicles with tape-recorded lectures, the culinary arts kitchens, and small group study—all provide more individualized instruction. Cultural relevance has also been added to the curriculum.

BIE reported that in 2011–12, Flandreau Indian Boarding School had a dropout rate of 36 percent and a graduation rate of 28 percent. In contrast, Riverside Indian School in Oklahoma had a dropout rate of 7 percent, and its graduation rate was 83 percent.[68] The urgent concern about dropout rates is not confined to BIE schools, of course; in 2011–12, Los Angeles Unified School District had a dropout rate of 21 percent and a graduation rate of 62 percent,[69] while California had a statewide dropout rate of 14 percent and a graduation rate of 76 percent.[70] The dropout rate of Sherman Indian High School was comparable at 10 percent, and the graduation rate was an astonishing 100 percent.[71] Supervising more than three hundred students residing and being educated on the campus of Sherman Indian High School is a challenge that is demanding and at the same time sensitive, but the dropout and graduation statistics are evidence that the Sherman administration and staff will have significant success in the endeavor.

Conclusion

Forgiving the Past

THE HISTORY OF SHERMAN INSTITUTE/INDIAN HIGH SCHOOL, as with all federal Indian off-reservation boarding schools, demonstrates the nineteenth-century legacies of Richard Henry Pratt and Thomas Jefferson Morgan, both of whom believed that white education was the only salvation for Indian people. Of the twenty-one presidential administrations during Sherman's history, nine reflected the assimilationist legacies: Grover Cleveland, William McKinley, Theodore Roosevelt, William Howard Taft, Woodrow Wilson, Warren Harding, Calvin Coolidge, Harry Truman, and Dwight Eisenhower. Conversely, the history of Sherman also manifests the self-determination legacies of Progressive reformers during the administrations of Herbert Hoover, Franklin D. Roosevelt, John Kennedy, Lyndon Johnson, Richard Nixon, Gerald Ford, Jimmy Carter, George H. W. Bush, and Bill Clinton. The presidential policies of Ronald Reagan and George W. Bush were equivocal: they used the rhetoric of self-determination but decreased the funding of BIE schools. Federally funded Indian schools were a focus of the administration of Barack Obama. Citing a history of mistreatment of Indians, he issued an executive order on June 26, 2013, establishing the White House Council on Native American Affairs. The order includes "expanding and improving lifelong educational opportunities for American Indians and Alaska Natives, while respecting demands for greater tribal control over tribal education."[1]

Sherman's twelve years in Perris, California (1892–1904), were a time of intense assimilationist efforts, which generated the extremely negative reputation of federal Indian boarding schools, a status reinforced by later assimilation policies. Sherman students endured coerced assimilation that demeaned their Native cultures and often involved severe punishment for their attempting to stay connected to their languages and traditions. The recent literature on federal Indian boarding schools recognizes that Indian children responded to their experiences in individual, distinctive ways.[2] There is, however, substantial evidence that the children had one response in common: ambivalence. My research on Sherman students shows them responding to forced assimilation by engaging in powerful moral confrontations, while navigating a middle course through ambivalence. Moreover, because self-determination is a complex mission and has limits, students in years of pro-self-determination also often found themselves in a demanding negotiation through a complicated middle course. How they coped corresponds to the concept of Christopher Boehm's dynamic ambivalence, responses determined by their social and cultural experiences and by the situation.

Despite the major positive changes of the Indian New Deal in the early 1930s, student labor was required to maintain Sherman Institute, which required finding a compromise between the strain of arduous work and the pressures of academic study. The fact that Sherman's Native arts and crafts program was needed as therapy for many students during the self-determination period of the early 1970s indicates that they may have been experiencing painful ambivalence even then. Despite liberal changes on the national level during the late 1970s, some Sherman students had serious problems negotiating the middle course between appreciating the Progressive aspects of the school and the "freedom" of drinking and smoking pot. In 1983, Sherman students evidently did not know how to handle some of the liberties afforded by self-determination. Having a curfew of midnight, most of them walked aimlessly up and down Magnolia Avenue, resulting in the curfew being changed to six P.M. in 1984.

From the opening of Sherman Institute, students were navigating this middle course. Romaldo La Chusa, a member of the first graduating class of 1904, expressed a strong attachment to the values of Sherman, but despite the assimilationist efforts to remove him from his culture, he declared, "I am proud to be an Indian." In *Education beyond the Mesas: Hopi Students at Sherman Institute, 1902–1929*, Matthew Sakiestewa Gilbert presents convincing evidence that Hopi students during the first two decades of Sherman history made accommodations that enabled them to succeed scholastically while maintaining the integrity of their Native culture. While students throughout the history of Sherman mainly accepted the powerfully imposed tenets of Christianity, many retained their traditional spiritual values, blending white and Native traditions. The Sherman cemetery, after years of neglect, was rededicated by local tribes in 2003 and reflects both Christian and Native spiritual values.

During World War I, Sherman students avoided the extremes of Indian warriors or disloyal draft resisters and joined the military for a myriad of personal reasons. Among the most dramatic depictions of students' successful negotiation of the middle course are the students who took their mastery of European classical music and instruments acquired at Sherman back to their reservations, adapting it to their own Indigenous musical expressions. The outing experience, originally designed to assimilate Indian children into mainstream society, unfortunately developed into a source of cheap labor for the community, but many Sherman students were able to negotiate a middle course. Most students valued the money they earned, and some came to be fond of their employers, appreciating their support in learning efforts.

Among the most painful moral confrontations were those of students such as Polingaysi Qoyawayma, who attended Sherman from 1906 to 1909, and Viola Martinez, who attended the school from 1927 to 1932. Both suffered alienation from their cultures but struggled valiantly to reconnect with their Native communities. Polingaysi, who taught in Indian schools, was able to blend the help from white friends and her own people to assist Hopi young people in attaining higher education.[3] Viola, who taught in Los Angeles public schools, was a founding director of the Los Angeles Indian Education Commission. As a revered elder, both in Los Angeles and in the Owens Valley, she confronted painful ambiguity by creating "new constructs from her familiarity with Indian and white, old and new."[4]

The students in the Navajo Program must have encountered myriad critical confrontations, being expected to master three years of white education in 120 days, to save them from a bleak life of incompetence in a modern world. Although one intention of the program was to avoid demeaning Navajo culture, there were gaps between intention and practice, revealing the persistence of ethnocentrism. Inadequately prepared administrators, instructors, and staff of the Navajo Program were themselves trying to find an appropriate middle course between the desire to make the program work and their anxiety about the demanding responsibility. Remarkable effort by both students and staff was required to relieve the instructors of the belief that the program was temporary and the good old days would return. Although the Navajo Program did not provide training applicable to the reservation, it did prepare students for urban employment. Despite the formidable requirements of the program, the ultimate achievement of the Navajo students is one of the notable successes of Sherman.

In assessing the successes of Sherman Institute/Indian High School, one has to acknowledge that the school is one of only four remaining of the original twenty-five federal Indian off-reservation boarding schools. The achievement is especially remarkable in light of the lack of adequate funding throughout its history. When it opened in 1902, funds were so minimal that students had to assume the responsibilities of administrators and instructors. Student labor was required to maintain the school even during the period of the Indian New Deal in the 1930s, requiring finding a middle course between hard physical labor and the demands of academic study. The Navajo Program, 1945 to 1960, was remarkably successful despite critically inadequate funding. Findings of deplorably inadequate funding of Indian boarding schools by the Meriam Report in 1928 were repeated in the Kennedy Report of 1969. As recently as 2009 and 2011, Sherman experienced devastating budget cuts that forced the school to lay off administrators, instructors, and staff, requiring those remaining to assume additional obligations. Although clearly overextended, they are committed to working hard to assure their students realistic opportunities for academic success, as evidenced by a dropout rate of 10 percent and a graduation rate of 100 percent, both superior to the California statewide rates and those of the Los Angeles Unified School District.

The degree of academic success apparent today is partly the consequence of Sherman's curriculum evolving from earlier half days of rudimentary academic studies and half days of vocational education, designed to teach Indian students "how to work." At the opening of

Sherman Institute, there was a strong ethnocentric focus on vocational education, an emphasis that continued to be reinforced throughout the assimilationist years. During the Indian New Deal, vocational education was designed to teach students skills appropriate for work in their Native communities. Today the education at Sherman Indian High School is designed to prepare Indian students for employment, but on a far more sophisticated level than the ethnocentric purpose of teaching them "how to work." Assisted by the generous and committed support of the San Manuel Band of Mission Indians, the Career Technical Education Program offers state-of-the-art training in five forward-looking career pathways, including bio-agriculture, alternative energy and resource management, health sciences, public services, and hospitality. Upon graduation, 25 percent of Sherman students attend college or trade school or secure jobs in their career pathway. After returning to their home communities for one or two years, more students enter college or trade school or find appropriate employment, raising the percentage to 35 percent.[5]

Sherman instructors and students credit the native culture programs, reviving deep-rooted native traditions, for much of the success. Lorene Sisquoc and Fern Charley-Baugus have been especially effective in helping students merge their Native cultures with their expanding contemporary technological environment. Sherman has also established exceptional intervention procedures for at-risk students, and the effectiveness of this program has contributed to the low dropout and high graduation rates. Students who have a history of substance abuse, previous difficulty in school, or other at-risk behavior have myriad options to remain at Sherman, recover, and attain a quality education. The Native culture and history components of the academic curriculum and extracurricular opportunities have diminished the alienation Indian students previously felt in BIA-funded Indian boarding schools.

Despite the transformations in federal Indian education policy reflected in off-reservation schools, scars from earlier years remain. Sherman students were not passive victims and often successfully negotiated a middle course, avoiding neither total assimilation nor rejection of white education, but finding the middle path required confronting painful moral choices. These confrontations have legacies that require healing.

CONCLUSION

A nationwide "Reconciliation Tour," organized by White Bison, an organization committed to helping Indian communities and individuals in need of healing, visited Sherman in 2009. Don Coyhis, president of the organization, argues that the high rates of alcoholism and suicide among Indians are the result of traumatic boarding school experiences. He stresses that healing begins with forgiveness. Lorene Sisquoc believes that retaining the off-reservation boarding schools is part of the healing process. She stresses that Sherman now has education and culture programs designed from the ground up, not imposed from the top down by the BIA: "We are changing what was forced on us to something we can benefit from. We are in a healing mode, forgiving the past."[6]

Should the federal government continue to fund off-reservation boarding schools? Those familiar with Indian education contend that many Indian students would not attend school without the option of going to one with an Indian-only student body. At Sherman, students may connect with their own traditions, while learning about many other Indian cultures. Leroy Miranda encountered stereotypes of Indians in a public school and believes he learned much at Sherman that he would not have learned in a non-Indian school. The success of Sherman Institute/Indian High School is best found in the testimonies of Indians such as Miranda who have a strong attachment to the school.

Miranda recalled, "Living at Sherman was probably the best experience of my life. I acquired a work ethic and self-reliance. I learned the importance of being Indian. My sister encouraged me to go because it was a very good school, and I am so glad she was right. I made many life-long friends at Sherman. I learned about many other Indian tribes. If it weren't for Sherman I wouldn't have gone to college." He voiced the recurrent, all-encompassing "I really enjoyed my years at Sherman."[7]

Students such as these undoubtedly will return for Sherman alumni reunions, keenly searching through the yearbooks, evoking memories of their experiences at the school, reconnecting with friendships made during their years there, and providing role models for students in the years to come.

Notes

Introduction: The Complicated Middle Course

1. Reyhner and Eder, *American Indian Education*, 150.
2. Trafzer, Keller, and Sisquoc, introduction to *Boarding School Blues*, 5.
3. Trafzer, Gilbert, and Sisquoc, introduction to *Indian School on Magnolia Avenue*, 1–18.
4. Lomawaima and McCarty, *To Remain an Indian*, 27–40.
5. Coleman, *American Indian Children*, 192.
6. Treuer, "As Long As the Grass."
7. Szasz, *Between Indian and White*, 6, 22, 23.
8. Ibid., 22.
9. White, *Middle Ground*, ix. Subsequent references to this work are cited in parentheses in the text.
10. University of Washington, "Richard White."
11. Usner, *Indians, Settlers, and Slaves*. Subsequent references to this work are cited in parentheses in the text.
12. University of Washington, "Richard White."
13. Birzer, "Middle Ground," 3. Subsequent references to this work are cited in parentheses in the text.
14. Quoted in ibid., 3.
15. Turner, "Significance of the Frontier." Available at http://sunnycv.com/steve/text/civ/turner.html, accessed February 18, 2013.
16. Lomawaima and McCarty, *To Remain an Indian*, 5, 173 (ch. 2, n. 2).
17. Trafzer and Loupe, "From Perris Indian School," 27.
18. Keller, *Empty Beds*, 2.
19. Szasz, *Education*, 9–10; Gilbert, *Education beyond the Mesas*, xxx; Reyhner and Eder, *American Indian Education*, 100, 142–45.
20. Quoted in Trafzer, Keller, and Sisquoc, *Boarding School Blues*, 206.
21. Child, *Boarding School Seasons*, 39–40; Coleman, *American Indian Children*, 86–88; Adams, *Education for Extinction*, 225; Medina, "Selling Patriotic Indians," 74.
22. Trafzer, Keller, and Sisquoc, introduction to *Boarding School Blues*, 22–23.
23. See Talayesva, *Sun Chief*; Qoyawayma, *No Turning Back*; Bahr, *Viola Martinez*.
24. Coleman, *American Indian Children*, 146.

25. Adams, *Education for Extinction*, 225.
26. Rosa Pace, correspondence with author, May 19, 2011.
27. Adams, "Beyond Bleakness," 223, 336; Trafzer, Keller, and Sisquoc, *Boarding School Blues*, 233.
28. Reyhner and Eder, *American Indian Education*, 207–209.
29. Ibid., 33.
30. Goldberg and Champagne, "Second Century of Dishonor," 320.
31. Szasz, *Education*, 37–40; Reyhner and Eder, *American Indian Education*, 245–46.
32. For an excellent account of the Navajo Program, see Elle, "Curriculum for Change."
33. Kennedy, *Indian Education*.
34. Ramona C. Bradley, "Sherman (Institute) Indian High School," document in Sherman Indian Museum Archive, n.d.
35. U.S. Department of Education, *ESEA Flexibility Request*, 21–24.
36. Ibid.

Chapter 1. Assimilation Imposed, Self-Determination Promised, 1892–1933

1. Lubo, "Early History of Sherman."
2. Holmes, "Sherman Institute," in *History of Riverside County*, 119; Rasmussen, "Institute."
3. Holmes, "Sherman Institute."
4. Quoted in Bradley, "Man with a Vision."
5. Lubo, "Early History of Sherman."
6. Holmes, "Sherman Institute"; Keller, *Empty Beds*, 91.
7. "Football Season Is Here," Sherman Institute Letters Sent, 1902–1948, NARA RG75.
8. Ibid.
9. All of the currency conversions in this volume are from www.usinflationcalculator.com using 2012 figures.
10. Sherman Institute Letters Sent, 1902–1948.
11. Ibid.
12. Quoted in Buford, *Native American Son*, 34.
13. Ibid., 45.
14. Ibid., 54.
15. Keller, *Empty Beds*, 138; Gilbert, *Education beyond the Mesas*, 83–84.
16. Buford, *Native American Son*, 54–55.
17. Ibid., 66–67.
18. McBeth, *Ethnic Identity*, 98.
19. Keller, *Empty Beds*, 63–64.
20. Gilbert, *Education beyond the Mesas*, 109.
21. Quoted in Holmes, *History of Riverside County*, 1.
22. Rathbun, "Hail Mary," 163.
23. Gilbert, *Education beyond the Mesas*, 72.

24. Sherman Indian Museum, "Sherman Indian High School History," www.shermanindianmuseum.org/sherman_hist.htm.

25. Adams, *Education for Extinction*, 62.

26. Gilbert, *Education beyond the Mesas*, 38, 48; "Sherman Institute Record of Enrollment," 120–80, Sherman Indian Museum, Riverside, Calif. (hereafter cited as "Sherman Indian Museum Archive"); Ramona Bradley, "Sherman (Institute) Indian High School History," Sherman Indian Museum Archive.

27. Adams, *Education for Extinction*, 138.

28. Ibid., 75.

29. Gilbert, *Education beyond the Mesas*, 139.

30. Bahr, *Viola Martinez*, 58–59.

31. Coleman, *American Indian Children*, 110–11.

32. Adams, *Education for Extinction*, 149; McBeth, *Ethnic Identity*, 89; Reyhner and Eder, *American Indian Education*, 132.

33. Keller, "When Native Foods," 2; *Indian Education Newsletter*, 1.

34. The construction cost was equivalent to $240 in 2012 currency.

35. *Indian Education Newsletter*, 5.

36. Paxton, "Learning Gender," 180.

37. Gilbert, *Education beyond the Mesas*, 84–85.

38. Adams, *Education for Extinction*, 157–62.

39. For a comprehensive account of the outing program at Sherman, see Whalen, "Labored Learning."

40. Gilbert, *Education beyond the Mesas*, 46–47; Paxton, "Learning Gender," 183; Trennert, "From Carlisle to Phoenix," 280.

41. Trennert, "From Carlisle to Phoenix"; Reyhner and Eder, *American Indian Education*, 139; Adams, "Beyond Bleakness," 47.

42. Adams, *Education for Extinction*, 163; Adams, "Beyond Bleakness," 47.

43. Bahr, *Viola Martinez*, 62–64.

44. Whalen, "Labored Learning," 123.

45. Ibid., 124.

46. Ibid., 130.

47. "Deserters," Records of Outing Agent Fred Long, 1917–1930, NARA Box 110.

48. Max Mazzetti, "A School of Many Champions, Sherman Institute, Riverside, California, 1901–1992" (1992), unpublished article, p. 3, Sherman Indian Museum Archive.

49. *School Code: Governing the Conduct of the Boys*, document, n.d., Sherman Indian Museum Archive.

50. Paxton, "Learning Gender," 174–86.

51. Ibid., 183.

52. "Rules to Govern Indian School Girls in Families," July 21, 1893, document, Sherman Indian Museum Archive.

53. McBeth, *Ethnic Identity*, 99.

54. Various issues of the *Sherman Bulletin*, esp. January 5, 1910.

55. Adams, *Education for Extinction*, 170–73.
56. Gilbert, *Education beyond the Mesas*, 129.
57. Mills, untitled student paper, January 23, 2001 (unpublished ms.), Sherman Indian Museum Archive. 1; Rasmussen, "Institute," B4.
58. Keller, *Empty Beds*, 75–76.
59. Ibid., 111.
60. Ibid., 8.
61. Keller, "When Native Foods."
62. Gilbert, *Education beyond the Mesas*, 129.
63. Bahr, *Viola Martinez*, 53.
64. Keller, *Empty Beds*, 41, 77.
65. The amount requested by Hall was the equivalent of $12,600 in 2012 currency.
66. Keller, *Empty Beds*, 34.
67. Ibid., 34, 63.
68. Ibid., 33.
69. Ibid., 62.
70. Gilbert, *Education beyond the Mesas*, 108.
71. Ibid., 83; Archuleta, Child, and Lomawaima, *Away from Home*, 69.
72. Trafzer, Keller, and Sisquoc, introduction, 27; Sherman Institute Records, Student Rosters and Dropouts, NARA Box 1 (125).
73. Gilbert, *Education beyond the Mesas*, 79; Archuleta, Child, and Lomawaima, *Away from Home*, 63.
74. Archuleta, Child, and Lomawaima, *Away from Home*, 64.
75. Gilbert, *Education beyond the Mesas*, 79.
76. Adams, *Education for Extinction*, 276–306; Coleman, *American Indian Children*, 180–87; Reyhner and Eder, *American Indian Education*, 198, 202.
77. Qoyawayma, *No Turning Back*, 69, 70.
78. Bahr, *Viola Martinez*, 85, 156.
79. Qoyawayma, *No Turning Back*, 174–77.
80. Bahr, "Never Give Up," 25.
81. Reyhner and Eder, *American Indian Education*, 106.
82. Ibid., 107.
83. Bruyneel, "Challenging American Boundaries," 40.
84. Institute for Government Research, *Problem of Indian Administration* (better known as the Meriam Report), 346. An electronic copy of the Meriam Report, scanned and digitized by Thomas R. Hopkins, is available as a PDF at www.cwu.edu/ectl/diversity/wastate/meriamreporteducation.pdf. Subsequent references to this digitized version are cited in the text by page numbers that correspond to the pagination in the original Meriam Report.
85. Child, *Boarding School Seasons*, 26.
86. Meriam Report, 390.
87. This transportation cost was equal to $247.60 in 2012 currency.

88. Child, *Boarding School Seasons,* 21, 85; Reyhner and Eder, *American Indian Education,* 209, 226.

89. Sherman Indian Museum, "Sherman Indian High School History."

Chapter 2. Reform, War, and Innovation, 1934–1952

1. Reyhner and Eder, *American Indian Education,* 209–10; Szasz, *Education,* 39.
2. Szasz, *Education,* 61.
3. *Sherman Bulletin,* "Commissioner Beatty Visits Sherman."
4. Reyhner and Eder, *American Indian Education,* 210.
5. National Relief Charities, "1930s Indian Education."
6. *Sherman Bulletin,* "Inter-tribal Council Formed."
7. For a comprehensive account of the history of the Johnson-O'Malley Act, see Szasz, *Education,* 94, 181–86.
8. Reyhner and Eder, *American Indian Education,* 226.
9. *Sherman Bulletin,* "Arts and Crafts Course."
10. Halstead, *Work—Study—Live.*
11. *Sherman Bulletin,* "NYA Students at Sherman."
12. Ibid., "WPA on Campus."
13. Ibid., "WPA Work." This Interior Department renovation was equal to $297,000 in 2012 currency.
14. Ibid., "WPA and Indian Service $25,000 Grant." This WPA/Indian Service renovation was equal to $413,000 in 2012 currency.
15. Ibid., "WPA Assisted by Sherman Boys."
16. Ibid., "Armistice Day."
17. Ibid., "Blackouts."
18. *Sherman Bulletin,* December 11, 1942.
19. *Sherman Bulletin,* "Sherman Donates 72 Tons."
20. Ibid., "Notice."
21. Ibid., "High Praise."
22. Ibid., "Flu Epidemic."
23. Ibid., "Rural Home Life Course."
24. Ibid., "Sherman Farm Leased."
25. Ibid., "Sherman to Commence Defense Training Course."
26. The tuition was equivalent to $234 in 2012 currency.
27. *Sherman Bulletin,* "Sherman to Commence Defense Training Course."
28. Ibid.
29. Ibid., "Indians Donate to War Effort." The Crow donation was the equivalent of $145,000 in 2012 currency, while the Klamath contribution was $2,183,922.
30. Matthew Sakiestewa Gilbert, "Hopi Code Talkers," http://beyondthemesas.com/2011/01/22/hopi-code-talkers-receive-honor.
31. Szasz, *Education,* 33.

32. Thompson, foreword, v.
33. Coombs, *Doorway toward the Light*, 6.
34. Ibid., 17.
35. Ibid., 43.
36. Ibid., 11.
37. Ibid., 47, 48, 173.
38. Norma C. Runyan, report to William W. Beatty on Navajo Program at Sherman Institute, p. 1, Mission Indian Agency, General Classified Files, 1920–1953, NARA Box 806.2. Hereafter cited as Runyan Report.
39. Reyhner and Eder, *American Indian Education*, 239–40.
40. Cleora C. Helbing, "Orientation Course in Everyday Living, Given at Sherman Institute, Riverside, California, Week of August 27–31, 1951," p. 2. Sherman Indian Museum Archive, Navajo Program Collection. The value of the wasted food was the equivalent of $620–967 in 2012 currency.
41. Coombs, *Doorway toward the Light*, 99.
42. Ibid., 62.
43. Ibid., 100.
44. Runyan Report.
45. Coombs, *Doorway toward the Light*, 55.
46. Runyan Report.
47. Coombs, *Doorway toward the Light*, 56.
48. Runyan Report.
49. Ibid.
50. Ibid.
51. Runyan, Hall, and McClure, *Report to Schools*, 35.
52. Ibid., 35, 2.
53. Ibid., 3.
54. Coombs, *Doorway toward the Light*, 35.
55. Runyan Report.
56. *Sherman Report on Navajo Program*, undated document, Sherman Indian Museum Archive, Navajo Collection.
57. Runyan Report.
58. Ibid.
59. Ibid.
60. Coombs, *Doorway toward the Light*, 116.
61. Runyan Report.
62. Coombs, *Doorway toward the Light*, 116.
63. Ibid., 158.
64. Ibid., 80.
65. Ibid., 161.
66. Ibid., 122.
67. Sherman Institute Student Case Files, 1907–1981, NARA Box 32.
68. Runyan, Hall, and McClure, *Report to Schools*, 20.
69. Coombs, *Doorway toward the Light*, 122.

70. Ibid.
71. Ibid.
72. Runyan Report.
73. McBeth, *Ethnic Identity*, 88–89.
74. Ille, "Curriculum for Social Change."
75. Evans, "Greetings," 2.
76. Coombs, *Doorway toward the Light*, 168.
77. Galen Townsend, interview with author, November 17, 2010.
78. Lorene Sisquoc, interview with author, November 3, 2010.
79. Townsend interview.
80. Keck, "Look Back at Sherman Wrestling."
81. Townsend interview.
82. Tonita Largo Glover, interview with author, November 10, 2010.
83. Ibid.; Lorene Sisquoc, interview with author, November 3, 2010.
84. Lorene Sisquoc, interviews with author, November 3, 2010, June 20, 2012.
85. Tonita Largo Glover interview.
86. Michele Meyers Conejo, interview with author, November 3, 2010. Michele is the godchild of Viola Martinez, who graduated from Sherman Institute in 1932 and whose life story is published in Bahr, *Viola Martinez*.
87. Willetta Davis Goins, interview with author, November 17, 2010; Jason Davis, interview with author, January 6, 2011.
88. Gary H. Evans, e-mail to author, January 11, 2011; Robert Evans, phone interview with author, January 25, 2011.
89. Conejo interview.
90. Goins interview.
91. Sherman Institute Student Rosters and Dropouts, NARA Box 1 (125).
92. Ibid.
93. Conejo, Glover, and Goins interviews; Jason Davis, phone interview with author, January 31, 2010; Melvin Campbell, interview with author, November 7, 2010.
94. Goins interview.
95. Bahr, *Viola Martinez*, 54–55.
96. Townsend, Glover, and Campbell interviews.
97. Individual Files, NARA Box 32.
98. Conejo interview.
99. Lorene Sisquoc interview, June 20, 2012.
100. Sherman Institute Student Rosters and Dropouts, NARA Box 1 (125).
101. Townsend interview; Robert Evans phone interview.
102. Lorene Sisquoc interview, June 20, 2012.
103. Frazier letter to Miss Hall, February 15, 1948, Sherman Institute Student Case Files, NARA Box 32.
104. Untitled, undated note by Ethelyn Miller, Sherman Institute Student Case Files, NARA Box 32.

105. Untitled reports, November 15, 1946, and March 28, 1947, Sherman Institute Student Case Files 1908–1981, NARA Box 330.
106. Jason Davis, e-mail to author, February 2, 2011; Conejo, Goins, and Townsend interviews.
107. Mission Indian Agency, General Classified Files, NARA Box 806.2.
108. Ibid.
109. Campbell, Conejo, Goins, and Glover interviews; Lorene Sisquoc interview, June 20, 2012.
110. Lorene Sisquoc interview, June 20, 2012.
111. Runyan Report.
112. Campbell, Conejo, and Robert Evans interviews; Gary Evans e-mail.
113. Lorene Sisquoc interview, June 20, 2010; Tonita Marie Maciel, e-mail to author, February 24, 2011.
114. Townsend and Goins interviews; Jason Davis, e-mail to author, February 2, 2011.
115. Campbell interview.
116. Conejo interview; Jason Davis e-mail to author, January 6, 2011.
117. Glover interview.
118. Lorene Sisquoc interview, June 20, 2012.
119. Gary Evans e-mail; Robert Evans interview.
120. Quoted in Reyhner and Eder, *American Indian Education*, 233–34.
121. Ibid., 241–43; Szasz, *Education*, 3.

Chapter 3. Termination—"Tragedy" and "Challenge," 1953–1972

1. Reyhner and Eder, *American Indian Education*, 135–36; National Relief Charities, "Termination Policy."
2. National Relief Charities, "Termination Policy."
3. Szasz, *Education*, 137–39.
4. Ibid.
5. *Sherman Indian High School Student Guide to Success*, 2. Hereafter cited as *SIHS Student Guide*.
6. Szasz, *Education*, 137–38.
7. *Sherman Bulletin*, "Commissioner of Indian Affairs Visits."
8. Ibid., "Half of Student Income Derived from Work."
9. The boys' and girls' September 1962 income was equivalent to $18,393 and $15,250, respectively, in 2012 currency. All the income and spending data in this paragraph are from ibid.
10. The boys' and girls' Save the Children Federation funding was equivalent to $7,313 and $4,246, respectively, in 2012 currency.
11. The girls' and boys' money sent from home was equivalent to $11,118 and $7,313, respectively, in 2012 currency.
12. The combined spending on clothing was equivalent to $17,419 in 2012 currency, with girls spending $2,876 more.

13. *Sherman Bulletin*, "Why I Like Sherman."
14. Szasz, *Education*, 139; Senese, *Self-Determination*, 72.
15. Szasz, *Education*, 183; Reyhner and Eder, *American Indian Education*, 244.
16. Szasz, *Education*, 184.
17. *Sherman Bulletin*, "Sherman Projects Funded."
18. Szasz, *Education*, 139; Senese, *Self-Determination*, 72.
19. Szasz, *Education*, 141; Senese, *Self-Determination*, 102.
20. Bennett and Coombs, "Effective Education," 21.
21. Quoted in Senese, *Self-Determination*, 141–42.
22. Szasz, *Education*, 141.
23. *Sherman Bulletin*, "Building Improvements Long Overdue."
24. Ibid.
25. The annual budget was the equivalent of $9,542,760 in 2012 currency.
26. *Arlington Times*, "Don't Forget Our Indians!" Student income was the equivalent of $340,813 in 2012 currency; student deposits, $204,488; and the Save the Children Federation, $74,979.
27. Addison, "Sherman Tent Seen Likely."
28. Ibid. The budget request was the equivalent of $272,650 in 2012 currency.
29. "Sherman Institute, Riverside, California, Assembly, January 5, 1968, Welcoming Members of the United States Senate Sub-Committee on Education," document in Sherman Indian Museum Archive.
30. Addison, "Senators Inspect Sherman Institute." The book budget was the equivalent of $39,669 in 2012 currency.
31. Ibid.
32. *Sherman Bulletin*, "Commissioner Receives Funds."
33. Szasz, *Education*, 150.
34. Kennedy, *Indian Education*, 3. Indian income was the equivalent of $9,917 in 2012 currency.
35. Ibid., 3, 4.
36. Szasz, *Education*, 150; Senese, *Self-Determination*, 97.
37. Reyhner and Eder, *American Indian Education*, 252–53; Senese, *Self-Determination*, 97; Szasz, *Education*, 150–52, 186.
38. Svenson, *Special Evaluation and Report*, 158. Subsequent references to this report are cited in the text by page numbers in parentheses.
39. Elwin Svenson, phone interview with author, September 27, 2011.
40. The Sherman Institute teacher salary was the equivalent of $38,228 in 2012 currency, while the Riverside salary was $42,447.
41. "Report on the Sherman Institute Conference, June 1969, Prepared by Mrs. Claire [sic] J. Taber on Behalf of Congressman John V. Tunney," in Svenson, *Special Evaluation and Report*, 166.
42. Svenson phone interview.

43. Ibid.
44. Dutschke and Santa Barbara Indian Center, "History of American Indians."
45. Ibid.
46. *Riverside Daily Enterprise*, "Robert L. Bennett."
47. Pollard, "New Image," B2, B4.
48. Ibid., B4.
49. *Riverside Daily Enterprise*, "School Made Dramatic Change."
50. Graze, "Despite Problems."
51. *Riverside Daily Enterprise*, "Many Helping Create."
52. Sherman Indian Museum, "History of Sherman Indian Museum," www.shermanindianmuseum.org/history3.htm, accessed February 6, 2012.
53. Capriccioso, "This Presidents' Day," February 20, 2012, available at http://indiancountrytodaymedianetwork.com/article/this-presidents-day-we-highlight-the-best-presidents-for-indian-country-98923.
54. Nixon, "Special Message to Congress."
55. Szasz, *Education*, 113.
56. This was the third Indian occupation of Alcatraz. In 1964, five Sioux Indians occupied the island for four hours, calling for Alcatraz to be transformed into a cultural center and Indian university, and on November 9, 1969, Mohawk Richard Oakes led fourteen Indians to occupy Alcatraz overnight. "The Native American Power Movement," *Digital History*, www.digitalhistory.uh.edu/disp_textbook.cfm?smtID=2&psid=3348; Olson-Raymer, "Red Power in California," discussion guidelines, http://users.humboldt.edu/ogayle/hist383/RedPower.html.

Chapter 4. Red Power and Self-Determination, 1973–2000

1. Reyhner and Eder, *American Indian Education*, 254, 257; Szasz, *Education*, 143.
2. *Alcatraz Is Not an Island*.
3. Guarino, "Sherman Sympathizes."
4. *Alcatraz Is Not an Island*.
5. U.S. Department of Health, Education and Welfare, National Institute of Education, "First Annual Report to Congress"; U.S. Department of Education, Office of Indian Education, "History of Indian Education"; Reyhner and Eder, *American Indian Education*, 254–55; Szasz, *Education*, 147–201.
6. *Arlington Times*, "Sherman Construction."
7. Ibid.
8. Guarino, "Academic Complex Transformation." The $3 million construction amount was equivalent to $17,006,963 in 2012 currency.
9. Ibid.
10. *Arlington Times* news clipping, untitled, undated, Sherman Indian Museum Archive.
11. Ibid.

12. *Sherman Indian High School Handbook*, 2. Subsequent references to this handbook are cited in the text by page numbers in parentheses.
13. *Sherman Bulletin*, "For Girls Only"; Lorene Sisquoc, e-mail to author, July 7, 2012.
14. Their earnings were equivalent to $281 in 2012 currency.
15. $304 in 2012 currency.
16. Kolb, "Indian Students." The sale price of the students' share was equivalent to $216 in 2012 currency.
17. J. Lloyd Trump, "How the Project Evolved and Developed," *NASSP Bulletin* 61 (November 1977): 1, http://bul.sagepub.com/content/61/412/extract; *Sherman Indian High School Handbook*, 27.
18. *Sherman Indian High School Braves Yearbook*, "1971–1972 Was a Very Good Year."
19. Szasz, *Education*, 141.
20. Fixico, "Arizona at 100 Years"; Ford, "Gerald Ford Statement."
21. *Sherman Bulletin*, "Superintendents Welcome Noel D. Scott."
22. Gale, "Indian Self-Determination and Education Assistance Act."
23. *Sherman Bulletin*, "Parents Meet on Campus."
24. High, *Sherman Indian High School*.
25. Ibid.
26. Ibid.
27. *Sherman Bulletin*, "Do You Think."
28. Cram, "Changes in Presidential Views and Actions toward Native Americans," April 17, 2011, http://amin210.wikispaces.com/Changes+in+presidential+views+and+actions+toward+native+americans.
29. Szasz, *Education*, 216–17.
30. Reyhner and Eder, *American Indian Education*, 283–88.
31. Ibid., 287.
32. Reyhner, "American Indian Cultures," 6.
33. Thull, "Legislation Following AIRFA."
34. Reyhner, "Plans for Dropout Prevention."
35. Ibid.
36. High, *Sherman Indian High School*.
37. Indian Nations at Risk Task Force, *Indian Nations at Risk*, 6–12.
38. The funding request was equivalent to $2,753,988 in 2012 currency.
39. Sahagun, "Indian School Gets Praise." In 2012 currency, the per-student cut was equivalent to $36.72.
40. Ibid.
41. The discrepancy between teacher salaries was equivalent to $14,844 in 2012 currency.
42. Sahagun, "Indian School Gets Praise," 18.
43. Ibid.
44. *Woodlake Echo*, "February 12 Dedication."
45. *Navajo Times*, "Physician"; Vigran, "Physician Frank Clarke."

46. Lorene Sisquoc, e-mail to author, July 20, 2012.
47. St. Germaine, "BIA Schools," 3, 4.
48. "New Proclamation! Taylor's Trail Proclamation," Sherman Indian High School Intertribal Council, April 30, 2011, www.facebook.com/notes/sherman-indian-museum/newproclamation/new-proclamation, accessed April 20, 2012.
49. U.S. Senate, "Performance," 30–31.
50. Petix, "Sherman Indian School."
51. St. Germaine, "BIA Schools," 6; Szasz, *Education*, 201.
52. Szasz, *Education*, 223–28, 231; Reyhner and Eder, *American Indian Education*, 318. The fund was equivalent to approximately $390,000,000 in 2012 currency.
53. *Riverside Press-Enterprise*, "Graduation."
54. Wisconsin Historical Society, "Ada Deer."
55. "Remarks of Kevin Gover."
56. Olson, "Reconciliation Sought."
57. McKinnon, "U.S. Offers an Official Apology," *Wall Street Journal, Washington Wire* blog, December 22, 2009, http://blogs.wsj.com/washwire/2009/12/22/us-offers-an-official-apology-to-native-americans.

Chapter 5. Self-Determination and At-Risk Students, 2001–2012

1. *National Native News*, "Headline Archives."
2. Diaz, "Ties to Gambling."
3. Falmouth Institute, "Artman Resigns," *American Indian Report: AIRBlog*, April 28, 2008, http://falmouth-air.blogspot.com/2008_04_01_archive.html.
4. U.S. Department of the Interior, "Assistant Secretary–Indian Affairs David Anderson."
5. UCR Newsroom, "New $1 Million Grant," http://newsroom.ucr.edu/866.
6. U.S. Department of Education, "Executive Summary," *Ed.gov*, "No Child Left Behind," http://www2.ed.gov/nclb/overview/intro/execsumm.html.
7. *Education Week*, "No Child Left Behind," August 4, 2004, pp. 1–3, www.edweek.org/ew/issues/no-child-left-behind.
8. Ibid.
9. Reyhner, "Creating Sacred Places," 19.
10. National Education Association, "NCLB Leaves Native American Students Behind," www.nea.org/home/17852.htm.
11. NYS Affirmative Action Advisory Council, "Native Languages Preservation Bill," www.nysaaac.org/native_american_affairs.htm.
12. *Porch Creek News* (Atmore, Ala.), "Native Language Act," 1, 3.
13. U.S. Department of Education, "26 More States," www.ed.gov/news/press-releases/26-more-states-and-dc-seek-flexibility-nclb-drive-education-reforms-second-round.
14. In April 2012, Echo Hawk retired and Del Laverdure was selected as acting director until Obama nominated Kevin Washburn in August to become assistant secretary of Indian Affairs of the Department of the Interior.

15. Capriccioso, "Obama Signs Executive Order," http://indiancountrytodaymedianetwork.com/article/obama-signs-executive-order-on-education-and-tribal-colleges.
16. Olson, "Sherman Indian High School," 1, 2; Parsavand, "Sherman Indian High School," 1–3.
17. Olson, "Sherman Indian High School," 1.
18. Ibid.
19. *SIHS Student Guide*, n.p.
20. Ibid.
21. Indianz.com, "Survey Finds High-Risk Behavior," www.indianz.com/News/archives/002518.asp.
22. Snyder and Associates, "Underage Drinking Statistics" (after National Institute on Alcohol Abuse and Alcoholism), www.edgarsnyder.com/drunk-driving/underage-drinking/underage-statistics.html.
23. Shaughnessy, Branum, and Everett-Jones, *Youth Risk Behavior Survey*, www.eric.ed.gov/PDFS/ED459056.pdf, p. 12.
24. Jacobs, "How Schools Can Help," http://ericdigests.org/2005-1/heal/htm.
25. "Disciplinary Process," in *SIHS Student Guide*, 2–27.
26. "Dress Code," in ibid., 31.
27. "Daily Flight Checks," in ibid., 30.
28. "Description of Referrals," in ibid., 24–27.
29. "Choice Program," in ibid., 16; "Choice Dorm Program," undated document in Sherman Indian Museum Archive.
30. "Disciplinary Process," in *SIHS Student Guide*, 25–26.
31. "Due Process," in ibid., 22–23.
32. "Zero Tolerance Behaviors," in ibid., 25–26.
33. Ibid.
34. Ibid., 2, 16, 17; Doepner, e-mail to author, July 2, 2012.
35. Informal discussion by author with Lorene Sisquoc, June 27, 2012.
36. Ibid.
37. Ibid.; *SIHS Student Guide*, 21.
38. *SIHS Student Guide*, 18.
39. National Coalition of STD Directors, "Promoting Sexual Health through STD Prevention," in Native STAND Curriculum, *Native STAND's Facilitator's Manual*, www.ncsddc.org/what-we-do/health-disparities/native-stand-curriculum; Doepner, e-mail to author, July 2, 2012.
40. Sherman Indian High School Holistic Health Program, *Mental Health Crisis Protocol*.
41. Sherman Indian Museum, "Welcome Back!!! Mr. Doepner," http://shermanindianmuseum.org/doepner.htm.
42. Legutki, "Multicultural Sea," www.ctap10.org/2006/11/15/multicultural-sea-ocean-suburbia.
43. Ibid.

44. San Manuel Band of Mission Indians, "San Manuel Band of Mission Indians Donates $2.5 Million for Career Training Academy at Sherman Indian High School," press release, May 13, 2010, Highland, Calif.

45. Ibid.

46. Ibid.; Riverside County Office of Education, "Sherman Indian High School Valedictorian," www.rcoe.k12.ca.us/newsroom/20110520_Sherman_Graduate.html; Riverside County Office of Education, "Unique Partnership," www.rcoe.k12.ca.us/newsroom/20100513_Sherman.html.

47. Riverside County Office of Education, "Unique Partnership," 2.

48. Doepner memo to parents forwarded by Sisquoc to author via e-mail, July 2, 2012.

49. Pala Band of Mission Indians, "Pala Giving Program," www.palatribe.com/programs/pala-giving-program.

50. California Baptist University, "Edison Grant," http://web1.calbaptist.edu/news/tutoring_program.aspx.

51. *Southwest Riverside News Network.com,* "So Cal Edison Donates to Science Project at Sherman Indian HS," December 27, 2011, www.swrnn.com/2011/12/27/so-cal-edison-donates-to-science-project-at-sherman-indan-hs.

52. U.S. Department of the Interior, Bureau of Indian Education, "Curriculum & Programming Update to Students and Parents," June 28, 2012, transmitted via e-mail to author by Lorene Sisquoc, July 2, 2012; *SIHS Student Guide,* 2.

53. *SIHS Student Guide,* 12.

54. Western University of Health Sciences, "Sherman Indian High School Students," www.westernu.edu/ladder-american-indian/news.php.

55. Southern California College of Optometry, "Students Receive Gift," December 14, 2010, available at www.scco.edu/index.php/happenings/happenings-news/year-2010.

56. Ibid., 1–2; Debra J. Marks, e-mail to author, March 27, 2012.

57. Jacobs, "How Schools Can Help," p. 3.

58. Lorene Sisquoc, interview with author, June 20, 2012.

59. Ibid.

60. High, *Sherman Indian High School.*

61. *Sherman Bulletin,* "Native Traditions Class"; Bear, "Indian School," www.npr.org/templates/story/story.php?storyId=17645287; Legutki, "Multicultural Sea," 1–5.

62. Doepner, e-mail to author, November 16, 2011.

63. High, *Sherman Indian High School.*

64. Reyhner, "Plans for Dropout Prevention."

65. Ledlow, "Cultural Discontinuity."

66. St. Germaine, "Drop-Out Rates," www.ericdigests.org/1996-2/indian.html.

67. Faircloth and Tippeconnic, "Dropout/Graduation Crisis," http://civilrightsproject.ucla.edu/research/k-12-education/school-dropouts/the-dropout-

graduation-crisis-among-american-indian-and-alaska-native-students-failure-to-respond-places-the-future-of-native-peoples-at-risk.

68. U.S. Bureau of Indian Education, Division of Performance and Accountability, "School Report Cards, SY 2010–2011, Sherman Indian High School."

69. Jones, "LAUSD Sees Fewer Drop-Outs."

70. *Daily Breeze* (Torrance, Calif.), "Drop-Out Rates Trending Down."

71. Doepner, e-mail to author, July 2, 2012.

Conclusion: Forgiving the Past

1. White House, Office of the Press Secretary, "Executive Order Establishing the White House Council on Native American Affairs," June 26, 2013, www.whitehouse.gov/the-press-office/2013/06/26/executive-order-establishing-white-house-council-native-american-affairs.

2. Gilbert, *Education beyond the Mesas*, 168; Adams, "Beyond Bleakness."

3. Qoyawayma, *No Turning Back*, 180.

4. Bahr, *Viola Martinez*, 157.

5. Sisquoc, interview with author, June 20, 2012.

6. Lorene Sisquoc, statement at research symposium, University of California–Riverside, May 11, 2012.

7. High, *Sherman Indian High School*.

Bibliography

Interviews and Correspondence

Interviews conducted by author at Sherman Indian Museum, Riverside, California, unless otherwise indicated.

Campbell, Melvin. November 7, 2010.
Conejo, Michelle Meyers. November 3, 2010.
Davis, Jason. Phone interviews with author, January 4, 25, 29, and 31, 2010; e-mails to author, February 2, 2010, January 6, 2011, February 2, 2011.
Doepner, Roland. E-mails to author, November 16, 2011, July 2, 2012.
Evans, Gary H. E-mail to author, January 11, 2011.
Evans, Robert. Phone interview with author, January 25, 2011.
Glover, Tonita Largo. November 10, 2010.
Goins, Willetta Davis. November 17, 2010.
Maciel, Tonita Marie. E-mail to author, February 24, 2011.
Marks, Debra J. E-mail to author, March 27, 2012.
Pace, Rosa M. Correspondence with author, May 19, 2011.
Sisquoc, Lorene. November 3, 2010, June 20, 2012; informal discussion with author June 27, 2012; e-mails to author, July 2, 7, 20, 2012; statement at research symposium, University of California–Riverside, May 11, 2012.
Svenson, Elwin. Phone interview with author, September 27, 2011.
Townsend, Galen. November 17, 2010.

Archives

Perris Valley Museum Historical Archives. http://perrisvalleyarchives.org/index.php?.
Records of Outing Agent Fred Long, 1917–1930. RG 75, Box 110. National Archives and Records Administration (cited as NARA in notes), Perris, California.
Sherman Institute and High School Records. Sherman Indian Museum, Riverside, California.
Sherman Institute Records. RG 75, Boxes 1 (125), 32, 300, and 806.2. National Archives and Records Administration (cited as NARA in notes), Pacific Region, Perris, California.

Secondary Sources

Adams, David Wallace. "Beyond Bleakness: The Brighter Side of Indian Boarding Schools, 1870–1940." In Trafzer, Keller, and Sisquoc, *Boarding School Blues*, 35–64.

———. *Education for Extinction: American Indians and the Boarding School Experience, 1875 to 1928*. Lawrence: University Press of Kansas, 1995.

Addison, Gordon. "Federal Aid Sought for Sherman." *Arlington Times*, November 1, 1967, p. 1.

———. "Senators Inspect Sherman Institute, Indian Heritage Training Stressed." *Arlington Times*, January 10, 1968, p. 1.

———. "Sherman Tent Seen Likely, Tunney Says." *Arlington Times*, November 1, 1967, p. 1.

Alcatraz Is Not an Island. PBS film, first broadcast November 7, 2002. Dir. James M. Fortier.

Archuleta, Margaret L., Brenda J. Child, and Tsianina Lomawaima, eds. *Away from Home: American Indian Boarding School Experiences*. Phoenix, Ariz.: Heard Museum, 2000.

Arlington Times. "Don't Forget Our Indians! Federal Aid for Sherman Sought from John Tunney." October 11, 1967, p. 1.

———. "Sherman Construction Enters Critical First Phase." November 29, 1972, p. 1.

Bahr, Diana Meyers. "Never Give Up: Viola Martinez Reflects on the Demise of the Los Angeles American Indian Education Commission." *News from Native California* 12, no. 2 (Winter 1998–99): 23–25.

———. *Viola Martinez: California Paiute Living in Two Worlds*. Norman: University of Oklahoma Press, 2003.

Bahr, Howard M. "An End to Invisibility." In *Native Americans Today: Sociological Perspectives*, edited by Howard M. Bahr, Bruce M. Chadwick, and Robert C. Day, 404–409. New York: Harper and Row, 1972.

Bear, Charla. "American Indian School a Far Cry from the Past." *Morning Edition*, NPR, May 13, 2008. Available at www.npr.org.

Bennett, Robert L., and L. Madison Coombs. "Effective Education to Meet Special Needs of Native Children." *Journal of American Indian Education* 3, no. 3 (May 1964): 21–25.

Bergstrom, Amy, Linda M. Cleary, and Thomas D. Peacock. *The Seventh Generation: Native Students Speak about Finding the Good Path*. ERIC no. ED472385. Charleston, W.Va.: ERIC Clearinghouse on Rural Education and Small Schools, 2003.

Birzer, Bradley J. "The Middle Ground: Historical Intermixing of Cultures." Blog post, July 30, 2012. Available at www.theimaginativeconservative.org.

Bradley, Ramona K. "Man with a Vision." *Arlington Times*, November 6, 1958, p. 18.

Bruyneel, Kevin. "Challenging American Boundaries: Indigenous People and the 'Gift' of U.S. Citizenship." *Studies in American Political Development* 18, no. 1 (2004): 30–43.

Buford, Kate. *Native American Son: The Life and Legend of Jim Thorpe*. New York: Alfred A. Knopf, 2010.

California Baptist University. "Edison Grant Supports CBU High School Tutoring Program," n.d. Available at http://web1.calbaptist.edu.

Capriccioso, Rob. "Obama Signs Executive Order on Education and Tribal Colleges." *Indian Country Today Media Network.com*, December 5, 2011. Available at http://indiancountrytodaymedianetwork.com.

———. "This Presidents' Day, We Highlight the Best Presidents for Indian Country." *Indian Country Today Media Network.com*, February 20, 2012. Available at http://indiancountrytodaymedianetwork.com.

Child, Brenda J. *Boarding School Seasons: American Indian Families, 1900–1940*. Lincoln: University of Nebraska Press, 2000.

Coleman, Michael C. *American Indian Children at School, 1850–1930*. Jackson: University Press of Mississippi, 1993.

Cook, Samuel. "What Is Indian Self-Determination?" *Red Ink* 3, no. 1 (May 1, 1994).

Coombs, L. Madison. *Doorway toward the Light: The Story of the Navajo Special Education Program*. Washington, D.C.: U.S. Bureau of Indian Affairs, U.S. Department of Health, Education and Welfare Office of Education, 1962.

Cram, Danielle. "Changes in Presidential Views and Actions toward Native Americans." April 17, 2011. Available at http://amin210.wikispaces.com.

Daily Breeze (Torrance, Calif.). "Drop-Out Rates Trending Down." June 28, 2012, p. 1.

Diaz, Kevin. "Ties to Gambling Haunts Anderson." *Star Tribune*, June 14, 2004, p. 1.

Dutschke, Dwight, and Santa Barbara Indian Center. "A History of American Indians in California: 1965–1980." In *Five Views: An Ethnic Historical Site Survey for California*. California Department of Parks and Recreation, Office of Historic Preservation, December 1988. www.nps.gov/history/history/online_books/5views/5views.htm.

Education Week. "No Child Left Behind." August 4, 2004, pp. 1–3.

Elle, Jon. "A Curriculum for Change: The Special Navajo Five Year Program, 1946–1961." In Trafzer, Gilbert, and Sisquoc, *Indian School on Magnolia Avenue*, 137–58.

Evans, Mythus. "Greetings." *Sherman Institute Yearbook, 1954*. Riverside, Calif.: Sherman Institute, 1954.

Faircloth, Susan C., and John W. Tippeconnic III. "The Dropout/Graduation Crisis among American Indian and Alaska Native Students." Los Angeles, Calif.: Civil Rights Project/Proyecto Derechos Civiles, January 1, 2010. Available at http://civilrightsproject.ucla.edu.

Falmouth Institute. "Artman Resigns." *American Indian Report, AIRBlog*, April 28, 2008. Available at http://falmouth-air.blogspot.com.

Fixico, Donald L. "Arizona at 100 Years of Progress and the Future." Arizona Convocation, March 4–5, 2007, Arizona State University, Tempe.

Ford, Gerald. "Gerald Ford Statement on the Signing of the Indian Self-Determination and Education Act." January 4, 1975. *American Presidency Project.* Available at www.presidency/ucsb.edu.

Gale. "Indian Self-Determination and Education Assistance Act." *Gale Encyclopedia of U.S. History*, n.d. Available at www.answers.com.

Gilbert, Matthew Sakiestewa. *Education beyond the Mesas: Hopi Students at Sherman Institute, 1902–1929.* Lincoln: University of Nebraska Press, 2010.

———. "Hopi Code Talkers Receive Honor." *Beyond the Mesas*, January 22, 2011. Available at http://beyondthemesas.com.

———. "Hopi Footraces and American Marathons, 1912–1930." *American Indian Quarterly* 62, no. 1 (March 2010): 77–101.

———. "Leupp, Francis Ellington." In "American Indian Heritage Month: Commemoration vs. Exploitation," *History and the Headlines*. ABC-CLIO, 2011. Available at www.historyandtheheadlines.abc-clio.com.

Goldberg, Carole, and Duane Champagne. "A Second Century of Dishonor: Federal Inequities and California Tribes." Report prepared by the UCLA American Indian Studies Center for the Advisory Council on California Indian Policy, March 27, 1996.

Graze, Gregory. "Despite Problems, Sherman High Has Made Much Progress." *Riverside Daily Enterprise*, December 18, 1972, B2, B4.

Guarino, Kathy. "Academic Complex Transformation." *Arlington Times*, March 4, 1973, p. 1.

———. "Sherman Sympathizes." *Arlington Times*, March 28, 1973, p. 1.

Halstead, Gordon. *Work—Study—Live: The Resident Youth Centers of the NYA.* Lima, N.Y., n.d. Available at New Deal Network, http://newdeal.feri.org/wsl.

High, Kat, producer. *Sherman Indian High School, 100 Years of Education and Native Pride.* Centennial commemorative video. Giveaway Songs Productions, 2001.

Holmes, Elmer Wallace. *History of Riverside County, California: With Biographical Sketches of the Leading Men and Women of the County Who Have Been Identified with Its Growth and Development from the Early Days to the Present.* Los Angeles: Historic Record Company, 1912.

Ille, Jon. "A Curriculum for Social Change: The Special Navajo Five-Year Program 1946–1961." In Trafzer, Gilbert, and Sisquoc, *Indian School on Magnolia Avenue*, 137–58.

Indian Education: A Fortnightly Field Letter of the Education Division, United States Office of Indian Affairs. Washington, D.C., April 15, 1941.

Indian Nations at Risk Task Force. *Indian Nations at Risk: An Educational Strategy for Action.* Final report. Washington, D.C.: U.S. Department of Education, October 1991.

Indianz.com: Your Internet Resource. "Survey Finds High-Risk Behaviors among BIA Students." November 13, 2003. Available at www.indianz.com.

Institute for Government Research. *The Problem of Indian Administration.* Also known as the "Meriam Report." Washington, D.C., February 21, 1928.

Jacobs, Don Trent. "How Schools Can Help Heal American Indian and Alaska Native Communities." ERIC no. 482350. *Eric Digests*, December 2003, www.ericdigests.org/2005-1/heal.htm.

Jones, Barbara. "LAUSD Sees Fewer Drop-Outs, but Graduation Rate Drops." *L.A. Daily News*, June 27, 2012, p. 1.

Keck, David. "A Look Back at Sherman Indian Wrestling." *Riverside Press-Enterprise*, January 25, 2011, B-1.

Keller, Jean. *Empty Beds: Indian Student Health at Sherman Institute, 1902–1922*. East Lansing: Michigan State University Press, 2002.

———. "When Native Foods Were Left Behind: Boarding School Nutrition and the Sherman Institute, 1902–1922." *News from Native California* 15, no. 3 (Spring 2002): 20–21.

Kennedy, Robert. *Indian Education: A National Tragedy, a National Challenge*. Washington, D.C.: Senate Committee on Labor and Public Welfare, 1969. www.tedna.org/pubs/Kennedy/introduction.pdf.

Kolb, Ron. "Indian Students Owned Part of GM." *Riverside Daily Enterprise*, May 13, 1974, B-2.

Ledlow, Susan. "Is Cultural Discontinuity an Adequate Explanation for Dropping Out?" *Journal of American Indian Education* 31, no. 3 (May 1992): 21–36.

Legutki, Gregg. "A Multicultural Sea in an Ocean of Suburbia." San Bernardino: California Technology Assistance Project, Region 10, November 15, 2006. Available at www.ctap10.org.

Lomawaima, K. Tsianina, and Teresa L. McCarty. *To Remain an Indian: Lessons in Democracy from a Century of Native American Education*. New York: Columbia University Teachers Press, 2006.

Lubo, Silvas. "Early History of Sherman." *Sherman Bulletin*, February 10, 1928, p. 5.

McBeth, Sally J. *Ethnic Identity and the Boarding School Experience of West-Central Oklahoma American Indians*. Lanham, Md.: University Press of America, 1983.

McKinnon, John D. "U.S. Offers an Official Apology to Native Americans." *Wall Street Journal, Washington Wire* blog, December 22, 2009. Available at http://blogs.wsj.com/washwire.

Medina, William O. "Selling Patriotic Indians at Sherman Institute during World War I." In Trafzer, Gilbert, and Sisquoc, *Indian School on Magnolia Avenue*, 65–77.

Miller Center, University of Virginia. "Grover Cleveland." In *American President: A Reference Resource*. Available at http//millercenter.org.

National Coalition of STD Directors. "Promoting Sexual Health through STD Prevention." In *Native STAND Curriculum, Facilitator's Manual*, n.d. Available at http:www.ncsddc.org.

National Education Association. "NCLB Leaves Native American Students Behind." October 2005. Available at www.nea.org.

National Native News. "Headline Archives." March 8, 2011, pp. 8, 23.

National Relief Charities. "The 1930s Indian Education Values Native Culture." In "History of Indian Education," American Indian Education Foundation, n.d. Available at www.nrcprograms.org.

———. "Termination Policy." In "History and Culture," Council of Indian Nations, n.d. Available at www.nrcprograms.org.

Navajo Times. "Physician at Phoenix Indian Hospital." January 10, 1985, p. 5.

Nixon, Richard. "Special Message to Congress on Indian Affairs." July 8, 1970. *American Presidency Project,* http://www.presidency.ucsb.edu/ws/?pid=2573.

NYS Affirmative Action Advisory Council. "Native Languages Preservation Bill Becomes Law." *Native American Affairs,* December 15, 2006. Available at http://www.nysaaac.org.

Olson, David. "Reconciliation Sought in U.S. Tour." *Riverside Press-Enterprise,* May 27, 2009, p. 1.

———. "Sherman Indian High School Faces Layoffs." *Riverside Press-Enterprise,* August 13, 2011, pp. 1, 2.

Olson-Raymer, Gayle. "Red Power in California." Discussion guidelines, n.d. Available at http://users.humboldt.edu.

Pala Band of Mission Indians. "Pala Giving Program." Pala, Calif., n.d. Available at www.palatribe.com.

Parsavand, Shirin. "Sherman Indian High School Copes with Recent Layoffs." *Riverside Press-Enterprise,* February 27, 2009, pp. 1–3.

Paxton, Katrina A. "Learning Gender: Female Students at the Sherman Institute, 1897–1925." In Trafzer, Keller, and Sisquoc, *Boarding School Blues,* 174–86.

Petix, Mark. "Sherman Indian School Wants to Be Seen, Heard." *Riverside Press-Enterprise,* November 25, 1995, pp. 1–4.

Philp, Kenneth R. "Dillon S. Myer and the Advent of Termination: 1950–1953." *Western Historical Quarterly* 19, no. 1 (January 1988): 37–59.

Pollard, Vic. "A New Image Is Goal for Indian School." *Riverside Daily Enterprise,* August 15, 1969, B2, B4.

Porch Creek News (Atmore, Ala.). "Native Language Act Ready for Bush's Signature." January 7, 2007.

Qoyawayma, Polingaysi [Elizabeth Q. White]. *No Turning Back: A Hopi Indian Woman's Struggle to Live in Two Worlds.* As told to Vada F. Carlson. Albuquerque: University of New Mexico Press, 1964.

Rasmussen, Cecilia. "Institute Tried to Drum 'Civilization' into Indian Youth." *Los Angeles Times,* February 23, 2003, B4.

Rathbun, Tanya L. "Hail Mary: The Catholic Experience at the Boniface Indian School." In Trafzer, Keller, and Sisquoc, *Boarding School Blues,* 155–73.

"Remarks of Kevin Gover, Assistant Secretary—Indian Affairs: Address to Tribal Leaders." *Journal of American Indian Education,* special issue 3, vol. 39, no. 2 (Winter 2000): 1–5.

Reyhner, Jon. "American Indian Cultures and School Success." *Journal of American Indian Education* 32, no. 1 (October 1992). http://jaie.asu.edu/v32/V32S1ame.htm.

———. "Creating Sacred Places for Children." *Indian Education Today* (March 2006): 19–20.

———. "Plans for Dropout Prevention and Special School Support Services for American Indian and Alaska Native Students." *American Indian Education* (January 1992): n.p. http://www2.nau.edu/jar/INAR.html.

Reyhner, Jon, and Jeanne Eder. *American Indian Education: A History*. Norman: University of Oklahoma Press, 2004.

Riverside County Office of Education. "Sherman Indian High School Valedictorian Chooses Medical Career Path." Riverside, Calif., May 20, 2011. Available at www.rcoe.k12.ca.us/newsroom.

———. "Unique Partnership among Riverside County Office of Education, Sherman Indian High School, and San Manuel Band of Mission Indians to Establish Career Pathways Program for Native American Students." Riverside, Calif., May 13, 2010. Available at www.rcoe.k12.ca.us/newsroom.

Riverside Daily Enterprise. "Many Helping Create New Indian Museum." October 20, 1970, B1, B3.

———. "Robert L. Bennett, Commissioner of Indian Affairs Visited Sherman." January 7, 1967, A1.

———. "School Made Dramatic Change." December 19, 1972, B2, B4.

Riverside Press-Enterprise. "Graduation." June 12, 1993, p. 4.

Runyan, Norma C., Martha Hall, and Florence McClure. *Report to Schools on Progress of the Special Program at Eight Off-Reservation Indian Schools, 1952–1953*. Washington, D.C.: Bureau of Indian Affairs, United States Department of the Interior, n.d.

Sahagun, Louis. "Indian School Gets Praise but No More Money." *Los Angeles Times*, March 28, 1989, p. 18.

San Manuel Band of Mission Indians. "San Manuel Band of Mission Indians Donates $2.5 Million for Career Training Academy at Sherman Indian High School." Press release, May 13, 2010. Highland, Calif.

Senese, Guy B. *Self-Determination and the Social Education of Native Americans*. New York: Praeger Publishers, 1991.

Shaughnessy, Lana, Cheryl Branum, and Sherry Everett-Jones. *Youth Risk Behavior Survey of High School Students Attending Bureau Funded Schools*. ERIC no. ED459056. Washington, D.C.: Bureau of Indian Affairs, Office of Indian Education Programs, 2001.

Sherman Bulletin. "Armistice Day." November 11, 1939, p. 2.

———. "Arts and Crafts Course." January 27, 1933, p. 1.

———. Beatty memo to Donald H. Biery (quoted). December 19, 1941, p. 2.

———. "Blackouts." December 19, 1941, p. 1.

———. "Building Improvements Long Overdue." October 18, 1967, p. 1.

———. "Cato Sells, Commissioner of Indian Affairs Visits." October 16, 1917, p. 1.

———. "Commissioner Beatty Visits Sherman." October 30, 1936, p. 1.

———. "Commissioner of Indian Affairs Visits." November 10, 1961, p. 1.

———. "Commissioner Receives Funds." January 30, 1968, p. 1.

———. "Do You Think Students Who Graduate Should Return to the Reservation?" May 8, 1981, p. 5.
———. "Flu Epidemic." November 26, 1940, p. 5.
———. "For Girls Only." November 5, 1982, p. 2.
———. "Half of Student Income Derived from Work." November 9, 1962, p. 1.
———. "High Praise Received by Sherman in 'Test Bombing.'" March 19, 1943, p. 1.
———. "Indian Definition Asked of Congress." December 16, 1932, p. 2.
———. "Indians Donate to War Effort." November 13, 1942, p. 1.
———. "Inter-tribal Council Formed." March 18, 1938, p. 1.
———. "Native Traditions Class." October 4–11, 2006, p. 2.
———. "Notice." March 19, 1943, p. 1.
———. "NYA Students at Sherman, ½ and ½ Days." November 19, 1937, p. 1.
———. "Parents Meet on Campus." October 17, 1980, p. 9.
———. "Popping Can Be Permanent." February 19, 1977, p. 3.
———. "The Prophylactic Quartette." June 2, 1915, p. 3.
———. "Rural Life Course." November 26, 1940, p. 1.
———. "School Auditorium Dedicated to Frank M. Conser." November 4, 1932, p. 1.
———. "Sherman Boys Fight Fire." December 2, 1938, p. 1.
———. "Sherman Dairy Wins Second Place." January 30, 1939, p. 3.
———. "Sherman Donates 72 Tons of Scrap Metal to War Production." November 13, 1942, p. 1.
———. "Sherman Farm Leased." March 19, 1943, p. 1.
———. "Sherman Girls Learn to Milk Cows." December 2, 1938, p. 2.
———. "Sherman Group Return from Extended Tour." September 16, 1927, p. 1.
———. "Sherman Projects Funded." September 9, 1971, p. 1.
———. "Sherman to Commence Defense Training Course." January 13, 1942, p. 1.
———. "Sherman Trains Welders for Defense." December 19, 1941, p. 1.
———. "Six Years Bring Big Changes." April 29, 1908, p. 1.
———. "Superintendents Welcome Noel D. Scott." September 12, 1979, p. 1.
———. "Table Manners." October 16, 1936, p. 1.
———. "Why I Like Sherman." April 8, 1962, p. 3.
———. "WPA and Indian Service $25,000 Grant." January 20, 1939, p. 1.
———. "WPA Assisted by Sherman Boys." October 13, 1939, p. 1.
———. "WPA on Campus." March 18, 1938, p. 1.
———. "WPA Work." October 13, 1939, p. 1.
Sherman Indian High School Braves Yearbook, 1971–1972. "1971–1972 Was a Very Good Year," p. 111. Riverside, Calif., 1972.
Sherman Indian High School Handbook, 1972–1973. Washington, D.C.: U.S. Department of the Interior, 1973.
Sherman Indian High School Holistic Health Program. *Mental Health Crisis Protocol.* Riverside, Calif., n.d.
Sherman Indian High School Student Guide to Success. Washington, D.C.: U.S. Department of the Interior, n.d.

Sherman Indian Museum. "History of Sherman Indian Museum." Riverside, Calif., n.d. Available at www.shermanindianmuseum.org.

———. "Sherman Indian High School History." Riverside, Calif., n.d. Available at www.shermanindianmuseum.org.

———. "Welcome Back!!! Mr. Doepner." Riverside, Calif., n.d. Available at http://shermanindianmuseum.org.

Snyder and Associates. "Underage Drinking Statistics" (after National Institute on Alcohol Abuse and Alcoholism), n.d. Available at www.edgarsnyder.com.

Southern California College of Optometry. "Students Receive Gift of Vision Care." Fullerton, Calif., December 14, 2010. Available at www.scco.edu.

Southwest Riverside News Network.com. "So Cal Edison Donates to Science Project at Sherman Indian HS." December 27, 2011. Available at www.swrnn.com.

St. Germaine, Richard. "BIA Schools Complete First Step of Reform Effort." *Journal of American Indian Education* 35, no. 1 (October 1995): 3–4. http://jaie.asu.edu/V35S1bia.htm.

———. "Drop-Out Rates among American Indian and Alaska Native Students: Beyond Cultural Discontinuity." *ERIC Digests*, November 1995. www.ericdigests.org/1996-2/indian.html.

Svenson, Elwin. *Special Evaluation and Report on Sherman Institute* (November 19, 1968). Vol. 3 of *A Compendium of Federal Boarding School Evaluations: The Education of American Indians*. Washington, D.C.: Congress of the United States, Senate Committee on Labor and Public Welfare, 1969.

Szasz, Margaret Connell. *Between Indian and White Worlds: The Cultural Broker*. Norman: University of Oklahoma Press, 2001.

———. *Education and the American Indian: The Road to Self Determination since 1928*. 3rd ed. Albuquerque: University of New Mexico Press, 2003.

Talayesva, Don. *Sun Chief: The Autobiography of a Hopi Indian*. Edited by Leo W. Simmons. New Haven, Conn.: Yale University Press, 1970.

Thompson, Hildegard. Foreword to Coombs, *Doorway Toward the Light*, v.

Thull, James. "Legislation Following AIRFA." In "American Indian Heritage Month: Commemoration vs. Exploitation," *History and the Headlines*. ABC-CLIO Schools, 2011. Available at www.historyandtheheadlines.abc.clio.com.

Trafzer, Clifford E., Matthew Sakiestewa Gilbert, and Lorene Sisquoc. Introduction to *Indian School on Magnolia Avenue*, 1–18.

———, eds. *The School on Magnolia Avenue: Voices and Images of Sherman Institute*. Corvallis: Oregon State University Press, 2012.

Trafzer, Clifford E., and Jean A. Keller. "Unforgettable Lives and Symbolic Voices: The Sherman School Cemetery." In Trafzer, Gilbert, and Sisquoc, *Indian School on Magnolia Avenue*, 159–72.

Trafzer, Clifford E., Jean A. Keller, and Lorene Sisquoc, eds. *Boarding School Blues: Revisiting American Indian Educational Experiences*. Lincoln: University of Nebraska Press, 2006.

Trafzer, Clifford E., Jean A. Keller, and Lorene Sisquoc. Introduction to Trafzer, Keller, and Sisquoc, *Boarding School Blues*, 1–33.

Trafzer, Clifford E., and Leleua Loupe. "From Perris Indian School to Sherman Institute." In Trafzer, Gilbert, and Sisquoc, *School on Magnolia Avenue*, 19–34.

Trennert, Robert A. "From Carlisle to Phoenix: The Rise and Fall of the Indian Outing System, 1878–1930." *Pacific Historical Review* 52, no. 3 (August 1983): 267–91.

Treuer, David. "As Long As the Grass Grows and the Poverty Shows." *Los Angeles Times*, May 20, 2012, A35.

Tribal Education Departments National Assembly. "National Advisory Council on Indian Education." Boulder, Colo., n.d. www.tedna.org/articles/nacie.htm.

Trump, J. Lloyd. "How the Project Evolved and Developed." *NASSP Bulletin* 61 (November 1977): 1–4. Available at http://bul.sagepub.com.

Turner, Frederick Jackson. "The Significance of the Frontier in American History." Paper presented at a meeting of the American Historical Association at 1893 World's Columbian Exposition, Chicago. Available at http://sunnycv.com/steve/text/civ/turner.html. Accessed February 18, 2013.

UCR Newsroom. "New $1 Million Grant to UC Riverside Strengthens Arts Outreach." *University of California, Riverside Newsroom*, August 11, 2004.

University of Washington, Office of Research. "Richard White and the New Western History," n.d. Available at www.washington.edu/research.

U.S. Bureau of Indian Education, Division of Performance and Accountability. "School Report Cards, SY 2010–2011, Sherman Indian High School," n.d. Available at www.bie.edu.

U.S. Department of Education. *ESEA Flexibility Request*. Washington, D.C., February 10, 2012.

———. "Executive Summary." *Ed.Gov*, "No Child Left Behind," n.d. Available at www2.ed.gov/nclb.

———. "26 More States and D.C. Seek Flexibility from NCLB to Drive Education Reforms in Second Round of Requests." *Ed.Gov*, February 29, 2012. Available at www.ed.gov/news.

U.S. Department of Education, Office of Indian Education. "History of Indian Education." Washington, D.C., n.d. Available at www2.ed.gov/about/offices.

U.S. Department of Health, Education and Welfare, National Institute of Education. "First Annual Report to Congress from National Advisory Council on Indian Education." Washington, D.C., 1974.

U.S. Department of the Interior. "Assistant Secretary–Indian Affairs David Anderson Brings Positive Message to Sherman Indian High School." *NEWS* (Washington, D.C.), March 17, 2004, p. 1.

———. *Report of the Commissioner of Indian Affairs to the Secretary of the Interior for the Fiscal Year Ended June 30, 1909*. Washington, D.C.: Government Printing Office, 1909. Digitized by the J. Willard Marriott Library, University of Utah.

U.S. Department of the Interior, Bureau of Indian Education. "Curriculum & Programming Update to Students and Parents." Washington, D.C., June 28, 2012.

U.S. National Library of Medicine. "Schools Must Keep Children Healthy, Commissioner States." In "Timeline, 1915," *Native Voices: Native Peoples' Concepts of Health and Illness.* Bethesda, Md., n.d. www.nlm.nih.gov/nativevoices/timeline/639.html.

Usner, Daniel H., Jr. *Indians, Settlers, and Slaves in a Frontier Exchange Economy: The Lower Mississippi Valley before 1783.* Published for the Omohundro Institute of Early American History and Culture, Williamsburg, Va.; Chapel Hill: University of North Carolina Press, 1992.

U.S. Senate. "Performance of Bureau of Indian Affairs Boarding Schools." In *Hearing before the Senate Committee on Indian Affairs, United States Senate One Hundred Third Congress,* 30–31. Washington, D.C.: U.S. Government Printing Office, 1995.

Vigran, Nancy. "Physician Frank Clarke." *Woodlake Echo,* November 17, 1993, p. 1.

Western University of Health Sciences. "Sherman Indian High School Students Added to Career Ladder." September 26, 2011. Available at www.westernu.edu.

Whalen, Kevin. "Labored Learning: The Outing System at Sherman Institute, 1902–1930." In Trafzer, Gilbert, and Sisquoc, *Indian School on Magnolia Avenue,* 107–36.

White, Richard. *The Middle Ground: Indians, Empires, and Republics in the Great Lakes Region, 1650–1815.* Cambridge: Cambridge University Press, 1991.

White House, Office of the Press Secretary. "Executive Order Establishing the White House Council on Native American Affairs." June 26, 2013. Available at www.whitehouse.gov.

Wisconsin Historical Society. "Ada Deer." *Topics in Wisconsin History,* n.d. www.wisconsinhistory.org/topics/deer.

Woodlake Echo. "February 12 Dedication at Sherman Indian High School." February 18, 1987, A-3.

Index

References to illustrations appear in italic type.

AA (Alcoholics Anonymous), 69, 124
Accelerated Reading Program, 127
ADD (Associate Deputy Director) offices of BIE, 13
Addison, Gordon, 76, 78
AIM (American Indian Movement), 89–91
Akimel O'odham (Pima Indians), 19
Alaskan Native (AN) education. *See* American Indian/Alaskan Native (AI/AN) education
Albuquerque Indian School (N.Mex.), 50
Alcatraz Island occupation, 87, 89, 150n56
Alcohol and drug use. *See* Drug and alcohol use
Alcoholics Anonymous (AA), 69, 124
Ambivalent responses to boarding school experience, 3, 4, 94, 136
American Indian/Alaskan Native (AI/AN) education: BIA schools for, 13; Cavazos's task force to evaluate, 99; EO by Obama to improve, 120; goals set by Clinton's EO 13096, 105; Rehner's recommendations for, 133–34
American Indian Defense Association, 33
American Indian Health Ladder, 130
American Indian Movement (AIM), 89–91
American Indian Religious Freedom Act (1978), 98, 105

Anderson, David W., 117
Apology to Native peoples by President Obama (2010), 107, 117
Apology to tribal leaders from BIA, 106, 117
Apple, Garfield, 121
Armed forces, and assimilationist/anti-assimilationist policies, 49
Artman, Carl J., 117
Assimilationist/anti-assimilationist policies, 43–44, 74–75; and armed forces, 49; and BIA, 9; of Perris Indian School, 135–36; postwar swing back to assimilation, 48–49, 72, 73; of Sherman Institute, 3, 31, 33
Associate Deputy Director (ADD) offices of BIE, 13
Association of American Indian Physicians, 102
Athletic programs: at Carlisle Indian Industrial School, 17–18; at Sherman Indian High School, 91, 103, 123, 125; at Sherman Institute, 17–19, 30
At-risk BIA students: and Choice Program, 123, 124; counseling of, 68; and disciplinary issues, 122–24; and Holistic Health Program, 126 27; and probationary students, 124–25; and realistic self-determination policy, 121; and STAND, 126; substance abuse of, 121–22; and zero tolerance behaviors, 96, 102, 124

Bahr, Diana Meyers, 8
Banks, Dennis, 91
Bannock, Shoshone, 61
Beatty, Willard W., 43, 47, 52
Beaulieu, David, 119
Begay, Victor, 125
Bennett, Robert L., 75, 76, 84–85
Bergstrom, Amy, 122
BIA (Bureau of Indian Affairs): AIM takeover of, 89; apology to tribal leaders on behalf of (2000), 106, 117; and Bennett, 75; building program of, 91; and Carlisle Indian Industrial School, 9; and debate over funding of Indian schools in twenty-first century, 14; and Effective Schools Monitoring and Evaluation model (1989–1994), 103, 105; goal of assimilation by, 9; and high school accreditation, 44; and Indian Reorganization Act of 1934, 11, 43, 54; and Indian Self-Determination and Education Assistance Act of 1975, 12–13, 95–96; and mismanagement of Indian affairs, 73; and Navajo Special Education Program, 12, 49; and problems uncovered in Indian education, 98–99; student attitudes toward, 90
BIA Brats: dating not permitted with students, 66; enhanced appreciation of diverse Indian cultures expressed by, 72; identity of, 60–61; idyllic life on Sherman campus by, 64–65, 66–67; jobs at Sherman held by, 69; negotiating the middle course by, 61; profound attachment to Sherman among, 61–62, 64, 70, 71; Riverside Public Schools attended by, 63; separation between students and, 65–66; Sherman as a safe haven for, 68. *See also* Campbell, Melvin; Conejo, Michele Meyers; Davis, Jason; Evans, Gary; Evans, Robert; Goins, Willetta Davis; Largo, Tonita; Sisquoc, Lorene; Townsend, Galen
BIE (Bureau of Indian Education) (formerly Office of Indian Education Programs): creation of Navajo Special Education Program by, 12–13; dropout and graduation rates reported by, 134; funding reduced for schools of, 135; offices of, 13; renaming of (2006), 13; schools funded by, 13–14; and STAND at Sherman in 2009, 126
Biery, Donald H., 45–46, 47–48
Bilingual Education Act (1968), 60
Birzer, Bradley J., 6
Blackhoop, Frank David, 31
Boarding School Blues (Trafzer, Keller, and Sisquoc, eds.), 10
Boarding schools: ambivalent student responses to, 3, 4, 94, 136; closing of, 33, 35, 98; complexity of experience, 14; discipline in, 9–11; and funding during World War II, 47; and Great Depression, 11, 35, 44; and homesickness, 10–11, 64–65; and manual labor required of students, 22, 34, 44, 136, 138; Native traditions suppressed at, 132; and student resistance to harsh discipline, 10. *See also* Assimilationist/anti-assimilationist policies; Kennedy Report (1969); Middle course concept; *names of specific schools*
Boehm, Christopher, 4, 136
Bradley, Judson M., diorama collection of, 86
Bradley, Ramona K., 63, 86
Brittain, Maurice, 64
Brittain, Naomi, 64, 65
Brophy, William A., 48
Brown, Eddie Frank, 99

Bruce, Louis, 89
Budget for Indian Affairs (2010; 2013), 119–20
Building projects for Sherman (1960s): and Bennett promise of support, 76–77; campaign by Tunney for new buildings, 76; Cecelia Charley's introduction of Kennedy, 77–78; construction completed in 1974, 91–92; and funds authorized by budget committee, 79; Kennedy's speech in support of, 78–79; restructured features of campus, 134; R. Kennedy and Fannin visit in support of, 77–78; Will Rogers, Jr., in support of, 76
Bureau of Indian Affairs. *See* BIA
Burson, Frank, 62
Bush, George H. W., 98, 99, 100, 135
Bush, George W., 117, 118, 119, 135

California Baptist University (CBU), 129
California Indian Education Association (CIEA), 84
Calvert, Ken, 104
Camp, Carter, 91
Campbell, Margaret, 65, 68–69
Campbell, Melvin: Coyote Valley Pomo and Second Mesa Hopi, 61; mother's love of Sherman, 68–69; on relaxed security at Sherman, 66
Campbell, Walter, 65
Career Technical Education Program, 127, 128, 139
Carlisle Indian Industrial School (Penn.): and alternating periods of assimilation and self-determination, 4; athletic program of, 17–18; and band, 30–31; founded by Pratt, 9; as model for BIA boarding schools, 9; and outing program, 23–24
Carlson, Vada F., 8
Carro, Milton, 62

Carson Indian School (Nev.; renamed Stewart Indian School), 50
Carter, Jimmy, 98, 135
Cavazos, Lauro F., 99, 101
CBU (California Baptist University), 129
Chamber of Commerce, Greater Riverside, 104
Charley, Cecelia, 77
Charley-Baugus, Fern, 131–32, 139
Chemawa Indian School (Ore.), 3, 50, 98
Cheyenne-Arapaho School (Okla.), 50
Chilocco Indian School (Okla.), 50
Choice Program, 123
Christianity, 9, 18, 28, 137
CIEA (California Indian Education Association), 84
Civil Rights Project of UCLA (2010), 133
Clarke, Frank, 102
Clarke Behavioral Health Center (later Clarke Cultural Center), 102
Cleary, Linda M., 122
Cleveland, Grover, 135
Clinton, Bill, 105, 135
Clinton Executive Order (EO) 13096 on American Indian and Alaska Native Education, 105
Co-educational Honor Dorm, 93
Coleman, Michael C., 4, 10, 21
Coleta, Taft, 25
Colley, Oscar B., collection of, 86
Collier, John, 11, 33, 35, 43
Community College Assistance Act (1978), 98
Conejo, Michele Meyers: BIA Brat interviewed by author, 61; on dances at Sherman, 66; on feeling of security at Sherman, 68; on friendships with students, 70; as godchild of Viola Martinez, 147n86; mother's satisfaction with Sherman, 69; on idyllic life on Sherman campus, 64; on making Indian friends, 71

Conser, Frank M., 16, 19, 21, 29–30
Coolidge, Calvin, 135
Coombs, L. Madison, 49, 75
Copernican theory, 22
Corena (Navajo student), 55
Coyhis, Don, 107, 140
Cronemeyer, Hoskie, 72
Culinary arts career pathway, *111*, 128–29
Culinary Arts Kitchen Lab, *111*, 129, 134
Cupeño and Luiseño Indians, 129
Curfew, 97, 136

Daily flight checks (DFCs), 122
Darrell, Unique, 128
Davis, Carl, 63, 120
Davis, Jason: found Sherman to be a safe haven, 67–68; grandson of Willetta Davis Goins, 61; homesickness of students reported by, 65; as Sherman counselor, 64; wants own son to work at Sherman, 71
Decoto, Ezra, 17
Deer, Ada, 105–106
Defense-training programs, 48
Deficiencies at Sherman, found by Swenson, 81–84
Department of Family and Community Medicine, 102
DFCs (daily flight checks), 122
Disciplinary issues at Sherman, 122–24
Distance learning, 127
Dodge, Chee, 72
Doepner, Roland "Tripp," *115*, 127, 129
Donaldson, Anthony, 129
Dormitories, *37*, 93, 120
Dress code at Sherman, 122
Dropout rates of Indian students: improvement today, 138–39; in Navajo Program, 54–55, 60; as rationale for Indian education investigation, 79; as reported by Reyhner, 100, 133; statistics on, 133–34
Drug and alcohol use: of BIA students, 121–22; and ISAAD, 98; of parents, 82; on reservations, 98; as result of boarding school trauma, 107, 140; and Sherman Indian High School, 94–97, 102, 123–24; and Sherman Institute, 67, 69; and STAND, 126
Duncan, Arne, 119

Eagle Feather, 132
Echo Hawk, Larry, 119–20, 152n14
Eder, Jeanne, 11, 98
Education Amendments Act (1978), 13
Education beyond the Mesas (Gilbert), 8, 19–20, 29, 136
Education Line Offices (ELO) of BIE, 13
Education Subcommittee on Labor and Public Welfare, 79
Educators, Native (tribal elders), 3–4
Effective Schools Monitoring and Evaluation model, 103, 105
Eisenhower, Dwight D., 73, 135
ELC (Eligibility in Local Context Program), 130
Elementary and Secondary Education Act (ESEA), 75
Eligibility in Local Context Program (ELC), 130
ELO (Education Line Offices) of BIE, 13
Emmons, Glenn L., 72, 73
Employment opportunities for students, 58–59
Empty Beds (Keller), 7–8, 29
Energy and Utilities Pathway, 129
English as a Second Language program, 127
English-only curriculum, 20–21, 72
ESEA (Elementary and Secondary Education Act), 75
Esther Martinez Native Languages Preservation Act (2006), 119

Ethnocentrism at Sherman Institute, 51
Evans, Gary: on friendships with students, 70; positive memories of growing up on campus, 64; son of Mythus Evans, 61; on sympathy with Indians' problems, 72
Evans, Mae, 64
Evans, Mythus: on academic progress of students, 78; making contacts for student employment, 58; and R. Kennedy visit, 77; sons as BIA Brats, 61; and teacher morale, 52, 54
Evans, Robert: on gaining appreciation for "people of color," 72; and memories of growing up on campus, 64; mischief of BIA Brats recalled by, 66; son of Mythus Evans, 61
Extracurricular activities at Sherman Institute, 31

Faircloth, Susan C., 133
Fannin, Paul, 75–76, 77, 78
Farm, school, 22, 23, 28, 29, 34, 47
Farming, 23
Ferris, Leslie, 62
Flandreau Indian (S.D.), 3, 98, 134
Flu epidemic (1940), 47
Forbes, Jack D., 84
Ford, Gerald R., 95, 98, 135
Fort Marion, 8
Frazier, Joe, 101
Frazier, Leonard, 67
Freeman, Clay, 46
Friends of Sherman Indian High School, 104
Frontier exchange economy, 5–6
Funding for Indian education: BIA debate over, 14; BIE and, 13; budget for 2013, 120; cuts under Reagan, 98; and decline in education effectiveness, 12; and facilities improvements, 29–30, 142n65; health-related request for, 29; and Meriam Report findings, 11; and Navajo Program, 50; as reported in *Indian Education*, 138; and Ryan investigation, 34–35; and Svenson report, 82; and Taber report, 83; and teacher salaries (1989), 101; testimony on, 103–104; and Title I, 75; during World War II, 47

Garment, Leonard, 91
Gerard, Forrest, 98
Gila River Reservation, 19
Gilbert, Matthew Sakiestewa, 8, 19–20, 29, 136
Girls/women: athletic program for, 19; code of conduct for, 26–28; and defense-training programs, 48; and domestic training and work, 22–23, 24, 26; and grooming, 53; indoctrination of at Sherman, 23; and music, 31; separate playgrounds for, 30; on Sherman Institute's Riverside campus, 40; vocational courses for, 55–57. See also Outing program
Giving Program of the Pala Band of Mission Indians, 129
Glover, Tonita Largo: annual Pow Wow started by, 125; on counseling at-risk students, 69; and four-generation history with Sherman, 62–63, 70; homesickness of students reported by, 65; mother of Lorene Sisquoc, 61; on need for education, 71; on separation of Brats from students, 65–66; work as counselor's aide, 63. See also Sisquoc, Lorene
Goals 2000: Educate America Act, 105
Goins, Willetta Davis: BIA Brat from Hualapai and Pala Reservation, 61, 67; on differences between BIA Brats and student schedules, 65; on feeling "special being Native," 71; Jason Davis grandson of, 67; on mother's love of Sherman, 69; Sherman described as "wonderful playground" by, 64; strong family attachment to Sherman, 64

Gover, Kevin, 105–106, 117
Grave, Peter, collection of, 86
Great Depression, 11, 35, 44
Green, Oliver, 91–92
Guarino, Kathy, 89–90

Hall, Harwood: and athletic program, 17; first hospital built by, 29; and funding requests to improve facilities, 29–30, 142n65; health concerns of, 15–16, 29; and outing program, 23–24; as proponent of English only, 21; and separation of sexes, 28; superintendent of Perris Indian School, 16
Hallett, William E., 98
Harding, Warren, 135
Haskell Indian Nations University, Lawrence, Kansas, 13
Helbing, Cleora C., 51
Hill, Lister, 79
Hogan, Webster, 77
Holistic Health Program, 126
Hoover, Herbert, 135
Hopi code talkers, 49
Hopi students, 19–20, 136–37
House Concurrent Resolution 108 (1953), 73
Howard, Edith, 86

Ickes, Harold, 43
Ille, Jon, 59
Indian activism. *See* Red Power movement
Indian Affairs budget: for 2010, 119; for 2013, 120
Indian boarding schools. *See* Boarding schools
Indian Citizenship Act (Snyder Act) (1924), 33
Indian Day, 86
Indian Education Act (1972), 91
Indian Education: A National Tragedy, a National Challenge (1969 report), 12, 81. *See also* Kennedy Report (1969)

Indian education investigation: and authorization to investigate boarding schools, 80; begun by committee headed by Kennedy, 79; dissatisfaction with Sherman reported in, 81–84; five fundamental principles of, 80; Kennedy rationale for, 79–80; recommendations by CIEA, 84; and summary report for, 81
Indian Health Service, 102, 124
Indian Nations at Risk (1991), 99–100
Indian Nations at Risk Task Force, 133
Indian New Deal, 43, 44, 136, 138, 139
Indian Reorganization Act (1934), 11, 43, 54
Indian School on Magnolia Avenue (Trafzer, Gilbert, and Sisquoc, eds.), 8
Indian Self-Determination and Education Assistance Act (1975), 13, 95–96
Indian Students against Drug Dependency (ISADD), 102
Intensive Residential Guidance (IRG) Program, 124–25
International, Edison, 129
IRG (Intensive Residential Guidance) Program, 124–25
Isabelle (Navajo student), 55
ISADD (Indian Students against Drug Dependency), 102

Jacobs, Wilbur R., 6
Johnson, Lyndon B., 60, 75, 98, 135
Johnson-O'Malley Act (1934), 43–44, 84, 96
Jones, Harold, 90
Journal of American Indian Education (1992), 133

Keller, Jean A., 7–8, 10, 29
Kennedy, Edward, 12, 80
Kennedy, John F., 74, 98, 135

Kennedy, Robert, 12, 75–76, 77–79
Kennedy Report (1969): inadequate funding reported in, 138; and Indian Education Act (1972), 91; and national debate on Indian education, 12–13; progress reported following, 100; Sherman harshly criticized in, 81–82
King-Johnson, Marilynn, 121
Knott, Frances, 130–31

La Chusa, Romaldo, 16, 38, 136
Largo, Ida Gooday, 62–63
Largo, Tonita, 125
Ledlow, Susan, 133
Leech Lake Reservation, 4
Leupp, Francis E., 29, 30, 33
Leveridge, Ron, 104
Levi, Robert, Jr., 100
Little Eagle Free, Inc., 130–31
Lomawaima, K. Tsianina, 4, 6
Long, Fred, 25
Longest Walk, 91
Lopez, Ray, 128
Lopez, Raymond, 121
Los Angeles American Indian Education Commission, 33, 137
Los Angeles Unified School District, dropout and graduation rates of, 134, 138
Loya, Robert, 101
Lubo, Silvas, 16, 17
Lujan, Manuel, Jr., 101

Maciel, Tonita Marie, 63
Marching bands, Sherman Institute, 30–31, 113
Marcoe, Beatrice, 10
Marine Corps Junior ROTC, 126
Marion, Jim, 92
Martinez, Esther, 119
Martinez, Viola: on culture changes from Anglo-oriented training, 32; and culture struggle, 137; on daily routine of school, 65; on illness at Sherman Institute, 29; as Los Angeles teacher, 32–33, 137; on Native language retention, 21; on outing program, 24
Mason, Don, collection of, 86
Maxwell H. Gluck Foundation, donation to University of California at Riverside, 117–18
Mazzetti, Max, 25
McCaleb, Neal A., 117
McCarty, Teresa L., 4, 6
McKinley, William, 135
McMorris, Jordan, 102
Meriam, Lewis, 33
Meriam Report (1928): effects on Indian affairs policy, 35; findings in, 11, 12, 34–35; findings repeated in Kennedy Report, 138; issuance of, 33–34, 144n84; and Navajo Special Education Program, 12; and Progressive anti-assimilation movement, 35; and severe criticisms of boarding schools, 34–35. *See also* Kennedy Report (1969)
Meyers, Emily Matsaw, 63–64, 65
Meyers, John, 63
Meyers, William, 63
Middle course concept: and BIA Brats, 61; contrasted with middle ground theory, 6–7; experienced by students from opening of Sherman, 136–37; and outing program, 24–25, 137; as response to complexity of boarding school experience, 14; as stated in student handbook, 92; and students returning to reservations with music, 137; and student struggles, 5, 10, 136, 139; and "turning the power" concept, 7. *See also* Middle ground theory
Middle Ground, The (White), 5
Middle ground theory, 5–6. *See also* Middle course concept
Military regimentation, 25–26, 30–31, 65
Miller, Ethelyn, 67

Miller, Frank, 15
Miller, Galene Townsend, 62
Miranda, Doreen, 97
Miranda, Leroy, 97, 100, 132–33, 140
Mission Indians, 19, 127–29, 139
Mission Inn (Riverside, Calif.), 15
Miss Sherman Pageant, 125
Mitchell, H. W., 17
Model School Project, 95
Montes, Josie, 102
Moorhead, Clara, 24
Morgan, Thomas Jefferson, 9, 20, 121, 135
Morse, Wayne, 79, 80, 81
Muscular Christianity, 18
Museum of the American Indian Act, 99
Music, 31–32, 137
Myer, Dillon S., 48–49, 72, 73

Nading, Harold, 86, *114*
NAGPRA (Native American Graves Protection and Repatriation Act), 99
Narcotics Anonymous, 124
Nash, Philleo, 72, 74, 75
Nasumgoens, 19
National Advisory Council on Indian Education, 91
National Congress of American Indians (NCAI), 75, 87
National Indian Education Association (NIEA), 119
National Youth Administration (NYA), 44–45
Native American Graves Protection and Repatriation Act (NAGPRA), 99
Native American Languages Act, 99
Native Daughters of the Golden West, 28–29
Native language: challenges in Navajo Program, 50–52; English only taught in early boarding schools, 21; and Esther Martinez Native Languages Preservation Act, 119; and loss of knowledge/fluency, 21, 100; in today's curriculum at Sherman, 14
Native Traditions Classroom, 131–32
Navajo code talkers, 49, 119
Navajo-Hopi Long-Range Rehabilitation Act (PL 81-474), 50
Navajo Special Education Program: and agriculture training on Sherman farm, 56; conservative demand to return to English only, 72; "crash" nature of, 59–60, 137–38; creation by BIA, 12, 49; and dropouts vs. "deserters," 54–55, 64; established in 1947–48 at three additional schools, 50; and ethnocentrism revealed, 51; evaluation of fifteen-year program, 59–60, 138; and high student morale, 54; and home economics, 56–57; and housing for student workers, 58–59; and job placement for students, 57–58; and language barriers, 51–52; and older students, 53; pilot program established at Sherman Institute, 49–50; problems encountered in, 52–53; students not literate in Native language, 50–52; success of, 138; teacher-interpreters needed for, 52; and vocational training, 55–57
NCAI (National Congress of American Indians), 75, 87
Nephew, Sam, 77
Nixon, Richard M., 87, 91, 98, 135
No Child Left Behind (NCLB) (Executive Order 13336), 118–19
North Fork Rancheria of Mono Indians, 84
Norton, Gale, 117
No Turning Back (Qoyawayma), 8
NYA (National Youth Administration), 44–45, 145n13

Obama, Barack: apology to Native peoples made by (2010), 107,

117; and creation of White House Council on Native American Affairs, 135; EO to improve education for AI/AN students (2011), 120; federally funded Indian schools as focus of, 135; waivers on NCLB authorized by, 119
Office of Indian Education Programs (later BIE), 9, 13, 72. *See also* BIE (Bureau of Indian Education)
Outing program, *110*; background of, 23–25; criticisms of in Meriam Report, 34–35; as extension of domestic training for girls, 26–27; major item in Pratt's agenda, 11, 23; as pool of cheap labor, 11, 24, 137; and runaways, 25; at Sherman Institute, 8; student income from in 1960s, 74

Pace, Rosa, 10
Pala Band of Mission Indians, 129
Parker, Ely, 75
Paxton, Katrina, 23, 26
Peacock, Thomas D., 122
Perris Indian School (Calif.), 36, 39–40, *110*; assimilationist efforts at, 135–36; Hall as superintendent of, 23–24; opening of Sherman Institute as, 3, 7–8, 15–16; outing system begun in, 26–27, *110*; students identified as Mission Indians, 19
Phoenix Indian School, 15–16, 23, 50
Pima Indians (Akimel O'odham), 19
Pine Ridge Reservation (S.D.), 89
Pocatello, Ray, 63
Pomona Health Career Ladder, Western University of Health Sciences, 130
Postwar Indian education policy, 49, 72
Pow Wow, annual, 125
Pratt, Richard Henry: background of, 8–9; coerced assimilationist policy as BIA model, 9–10, 20, 121, 135; and football program, 17–18; founder of Carlisle Indian Industrial School, 9; and outing system, 11, 23–24
Presidential legacies on Indian affairs, 135
Problem of Indian Administration, The. See Meriam Report (1928)

Qoyawayma, Polingaysi, 8, 32, 137

Rainy Mountain Boarding School (Okla.), 21
Ramos, James, 128
Reagan, Ronald, 98, 101, 135
"Reconciliation Tour," 106–107, 140
Red Power movement: and Alcatraz Island occupation, 87, 89, 150n56; BIA headquarters takeover by AIM, 89; and Longest Walk, 91; Wounded Knee occupation by AIM members, 89–91
Reed, Reagan, 93–94
Rega, Elizabeth, 130
Reifel, Benjamin, 95
Religious Freedom Act, American Indian (1978), 98, 105
Report on BIA Education (1988) (Reyhner and Eder), 98–99
Reyhner, Jon: on American Indian/Alaska Native education, 133; on critical dropout rate of Indian students, 100; on criticism affecting Indian policy, 11; on effects of NCLB on Indian schools, 118; and *Report on BIA Education*, 11, 98; on turnover rate for BIA professionals, 98
Rhodes, Al, 78
Risling, David, 84
Riverside County Office of Education, 128, 129
Riverside Defense Council, 46–47
Riverside Indian School (Okla.), 3, 98, 134

Robitzer, Ned T., 86, 91
Rockefeller Foundation, 33
Rogers, Will, Jr., 76
Rogers, Will, Sr., 76
Roosevelt, Franklin D., 43, 135
Roosevelt, Theodore, 18, 135
"Rules to Govern Indian School Girls in Families," 27
Runyan, Norma C., 52–53, 55
Rural Home Life course, 47, *112*
Ryan, W. Carson, Jr., 33, 34–35

Sakiestewa, Matthew, 8
San Bernardino and Riverside County Indian Health Services, 126
Sanderson, Leonard, 62
San Manuel Band of Serrano Mission Indians, 127–29, 139
Savage, M. H., 26–27
Save the Children Federation, 74, 76
SCCO (Southern California College of Optometry), 130–31
School Code: Governing the Conduct of the Boys (Sherman Institute), 26
Scott, Noel D., 85–86, 91, 96
Scribner, Willis, 62
Selective Service, Indians and, 48
Self-determination: and Alcatraz Island occupation, 87, 89, 150n56; alternating with periods of assimilation, 4–5; Bennett's promotion of, 75; and dependence on education, 96; educational gains made, 1933–1945, 11; and Indian Education Act (1972), 91; and Indian Reorganization Act of 1934, 43; Indian Self-Determination and Education Assistance Act (1975), 13, 95–96; Nixon's advocacy of, 87; and revitalization after Kennedy Report (1968), 12–13; and Sherman Indian High School, 92–93; and Sherman student council formed (1938), 44; U.S. presidents in support of, 98
Sells, Cato, 33

Senate Special Subcommittee on Indian Education, 77
Serrano Indians, 127
Seventh Generation, The (Bergstrom, Cleary, and Peacock), 122, 131
Shepherd, Ruby, 95
Sherman, James Schoolcraft, 16
Sherman Alumni Association, 25
Sherman Bulletin, 28, 44–45, 52, 79, 86, 94, 96
Sherman cemetery, 28–29, 137
Sherman Indian Foundation, 128
Sherman Indian High School: accreditation of (1971), 12, 74, 91; athletic program of, 91, 103, 123, 125; at-risk students, 121; and benefits during Clinton administration (1993–2001), 105; board members of, 121; campuses of, *41*, *42*; career pathways offered, 128, 129–30, 139; and Clarke Behavioral Health Center (1987), 102; classroom in 1963, *114*; and Co-educational Honor Dorm, 93; and curfew change, 97, 136; curriculum of, 14, 74, 134, 139; and disciplinary issues, 122–24; dropout and graduation rates of, 134, 138, 139; and effects of Goals 2000 Act, 105; and enrollment increase under Taylor, 104–105; and funding cuts in 2009, 120; funding not forthcoming for teacher salaries (1989), 101; and General Motors stock project, 93–94; low profile in Riverside community, 104; and Model School Project, 95; Native languages encouraged in, 14, 131; and Native Traditions Classroom, 131–32; and NCLB legislation, 118; philosophy and vision statements of, 121; praised as asset to community (1995), 105; and Scott administration, 85–86, 91; and self-determination policy, 92–93,

121, 122; six-year accreditation by WASC (1995), 105; social behavior required in, 94; and student attitudes on BIA, 90; student impressions of (1980), 96–98; successes of, 138; tribal affiliations represented in, 132–33; violations and demerits, 123–24; and Wounded Knee occupation, 89–90; and zero tolerance behaviors, 96, 102, 124. *See also* Building projects for Sherman (1960s); Drug and alcohol use; Sherman Institute

Sherman Indian High School Career Partnership, 129

Sherman Indian High School Handbook, 93, 94

Sherman Indian High School Marine Cadets, 126

Sherman Indian High School Student Guide to Success, 121, 122

Sherman Indian Museum, 41, 69; designers of, 86; and Galen Townsend, 71; Kennedy speech housed in, 77; and Lorene Sisquoc, 63, 115; and Margaret Campbell, 68–69; as Riverside Cultural Heritage Landmark, 86–87; trophies on exhibit in, 18, 86

Sherman Institute, 36, 40; alumni reunion of, 3; annual budget of, 149n25; beginning as Perris Indian School, 7–8; campus bakery, 56, 111; deficiencies found in, 34–35, 81–84, 138; dropout rate of, 54–55; ethnocentrism of staff, 51, 146n40; feeding of boarding school children, 34; first graduating class (1904), 16, 38, 136; and health issues, 29; and high student morale in 1960s, 74; opening of, 3, 15; peak student population of, 35; and playgrounds, 30; and Riverside community, 19; and Rural Home Life course for females, 47, 112; as safe environment for students, 68; and "separate spheres" for males and females, 28; and *Sherman Bulletin*'s role, 28, 51; student council of, 44; student labor at, 44, 136, 138; and tutoring program from CBU, 129. *See also* BIA Brats; Boarding schools; Navajo Special Education Program; Sherman Indian High School

Sherman ranch (1930s and 1940s), 109

Shingoitewa, LeRoy, 49

"Significance of the Frontier in American History, The" (Turner), 6

Simmons, Leo W., 8

Sisk, Calvin, 62

Sisquoc, Lorene, 115; *Boarding School Blues* (ed.), 10; as Clarke Cultural Center volunteer, 102; curator of Sherman Indian Museum, 63; on forgiving the past, 140; and four-generation history with Sherman, 62, 70; *Indian School on Magnolia Avenue* (ed.), 8; matron of boys' dorm, 69; on multilayered attachment to boarding school, 71; and Native culture program, 132, 139; as naughty girl, 66–67; on Sherman as "our reservation," 61, 73

Smith, Kenneth L., 98

Snyder Act (Indian Citizenship Act) (1924), 33

Southern California College of Optometry (SCCO), 130–31

Southwestern Indian Polytechnic Institute in Albuquerque, N.Mex., 13

Special Senate Subcommittee on Indian Education, 12

Special Subcommittee on Indian Education, 79–80, 81

Sports programs. *See* Athletic programs

SST (Student Study Team), 126

STAND (Students Together Against Negative Decisions), 126

INDEX 179

Stewart Indian School (Nev.) (formerly Carson Indian School), 50
St. Germaine, Richard, 133
Student income in 1960s, 74, 148nn9–12
Students Together Against Negative Decisions (STAND), 126
Student Study Team (SST), 126
Suicide, 107, 122, 126, 140
Sun Chief (Talayesva; ed. Simmons), 8
Svenson, Elwin, 81–84
Swimmer, Ross, 98
Szasz, Margaret Connell, 5, 98

Taber, Clare J., 83
Taft, William Howard, 16, 135
Talayesva, Don, 8
Talking Circle Room, 132
Tanner, A. C., 16
Tawaquaptewa, 19–20, 32
Taylor, Ken, 103–105
"Taylor's Trail," 104
Termination and relocation policy: continuation under Emmons, 73; decline under Kennedy, 74–75; education of Indians affected by, 73–74; focus after war, 11–12; Nixon's opposition to, 87; urban ghettos created by, 73
Thom, Mike, 90
Thompson, Hildegard, 55, 72, 73–74
Thompson, Morris, 95
Tinling, Steve, 101
Tippeconnic, John W., III, 133
Title I funding for Sherman, 75
Tohono O'odham (Papago), 48, 50
To Remain an Indian (Lomawaima and McCarty), 4, 6
Townsend, Galen: on BIA Brats on campus in summer, 66; disappointment at not being a Sherman student, 62; on Navajo students' arrival, 61; on playing basketball with students, 65; and pride in family history at Sherman, 62, 70; on sense of security on campus, 68; as teacher of arts and crafts, 62; as volunteer in Sherman Museum, 71
Townsend, Laura Premo, 62
Townsend, Matthew, 62
Townsend, Reggie, 62
Townsend, Ross, 62
Trafzer, Clifford E., 7, 8, 10
Treuer, David, 4–5
Truman, Harry S., 48, 73, 135
Tunney, John V., 75–76, 83
Turner, Frederick Jackson, 6
"Turning the power" concept, 7

Udall, Stewart, 75
Usner, Daniel H., Jr., 5

Valentine, Robert G., 29
Viola Martinez (Bahr), 8
Vision Care Day, 130–31
Vocational training, *112, 113*; and child labor, 34; and defense industry during war, 47–48; designed to prepare students for white society, 9; in eighth (and final) grade, 20; for girls and women, 56–57; inadequacy of, 82, 90; and Navajo Special Education Program, 49, 55–57, 60; strong emphasis on, 22–23, 138–39. *See also* Outing program

Wagner, Gladys P., collection of, 86
Warner, Pop, 17, 18
Warner, William J., 17
War on Poverty, 60
WASC (Western Association of Schools and Colleges), 105
Western University of Health Sciences, Pomona Health Career Ladder, 130
Whalen, Kevin, 24
White, Richard, 5, 6
White Bison organization, 106–107, 140

White House Council on Native
  American Affairs, 135
Whitman, Ivan "Rocky," 121
Wilson, Richard, 89
Wilson, Woodrow, 135
Women/girls. *See* Girls/women
Work, Hubert, 11, 33
Works Progress Administration
  (WPA), 44–45
World War I, 33, 137
World War II, 45–47, 48
Wounded Knee occupation by AIM
  members (Feb. 1973), 89–91

WPA (Works Progress
  Administration), 44–45
WPA/NYA at Sherman Institute,
  44–45, 145n13
Wyakett, Cynthia, 90

Yazzi, Joanne, 90
Young, Kenneth M., 128

Zero tolerance behaviors, 96, 102, 124

www.ingramcontent.com/pod-product-compliance
Lightning Source LLC
Chambersburg PA
CBHW020800160426
43192CB00006B/394